FOR ORGANS, PIANOS & ELECTRONIC KEYBOARDS

E-Z PLAY® TODAY

163

THE VERY BEST OF the Rat Pack

ISBN 978-1-61780-365-9

HAL•LEONARD®
CORPORATION

7777 W. BLUEMOUND RD. P.O. BOX 13819 MILWAUKEE, WI 53213

E-Z Play® Today Music Notation © 1975 Hal Leonard Corporation
E-Z Play and Easy Electronic Keyboard music are registered trademarks of Hal Leonard Corporation

Visit Hal Leonard Online at
www.halleonard.com

Come Fly with Me

Registration 4
Rhythm: Swing

Words by Sammy Cahn
Music by James Van Heusen

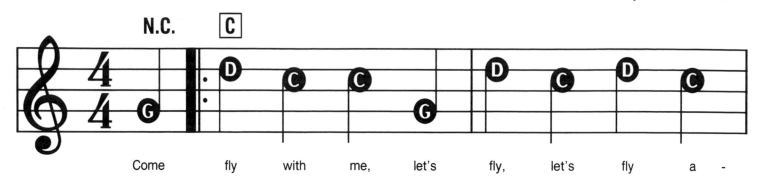

Come fly with me, let's fly, let's fly a -

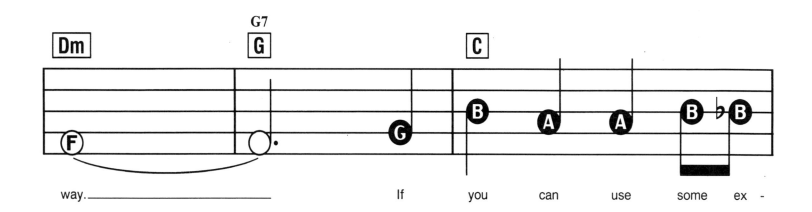

way._____ If you can use some ex -

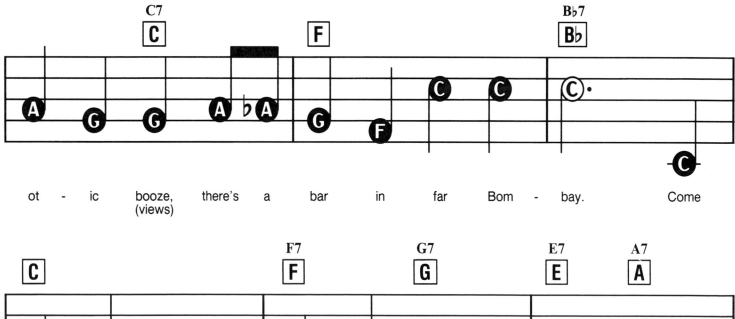

ot - ic booze, there's a bar in far Bom - bay. Come
(views)

fly with me, let's fly, let's fly a - way._____

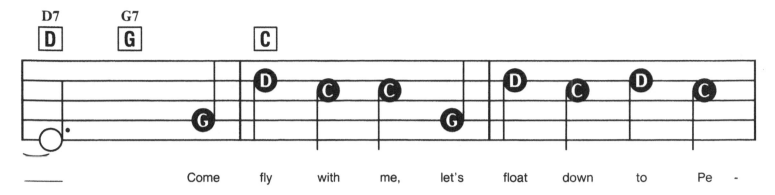

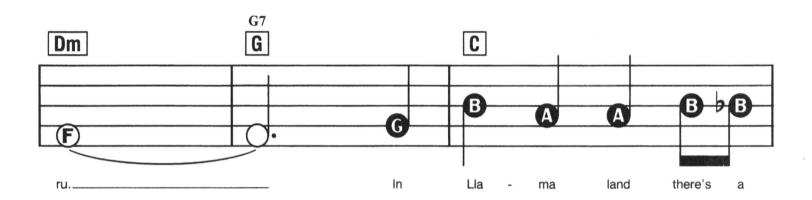

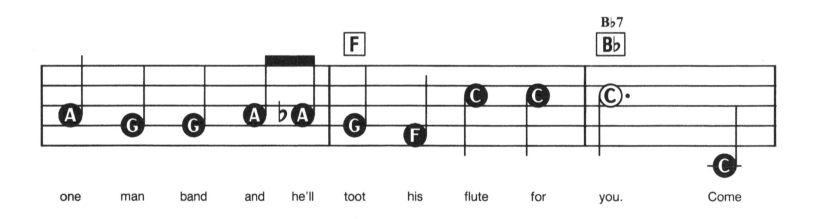

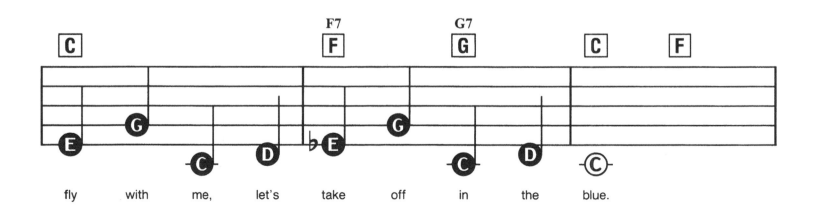

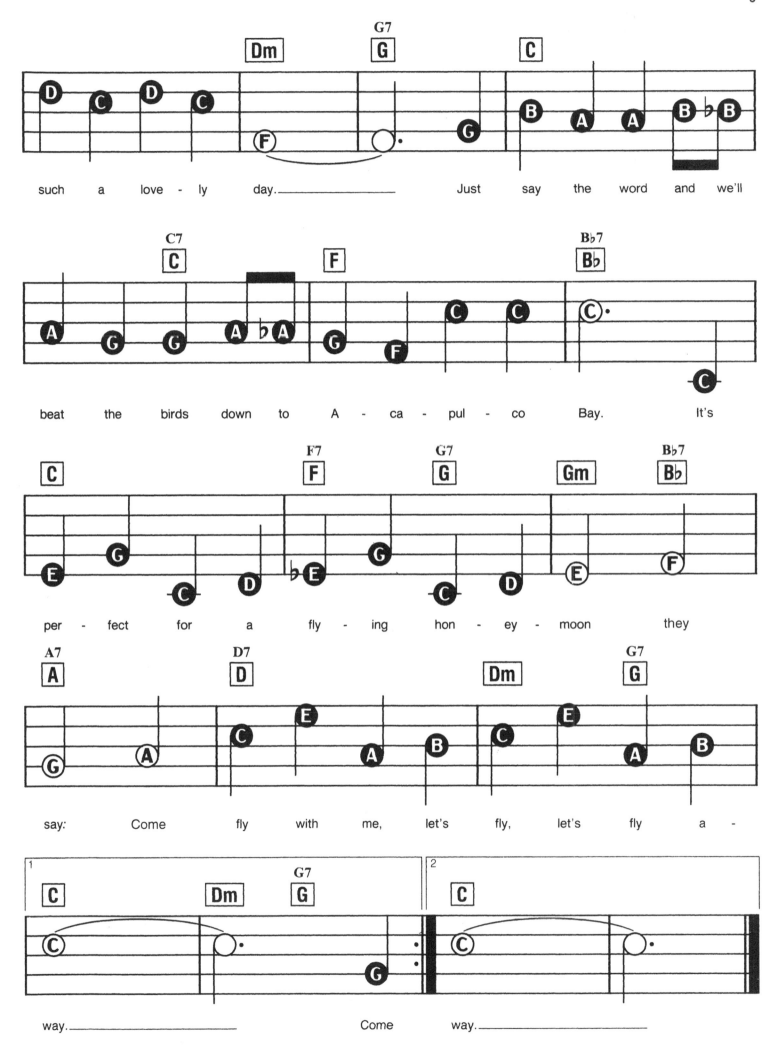

Ain't That a Kick in the Head

Registration 2
Rhythm: Swing or Fox Trot

Words by Sammy Cahn
Music by James Van Heusen

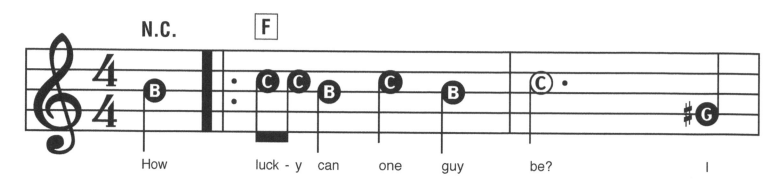

How luck-y can one guy be? I

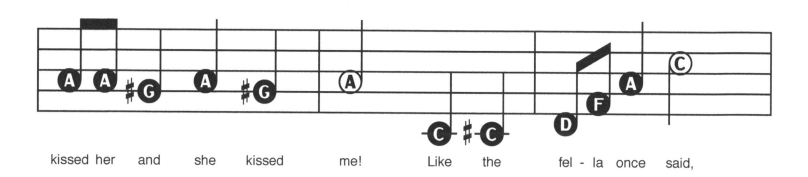

kissed her and she kissed me! Like the fel-la once said,

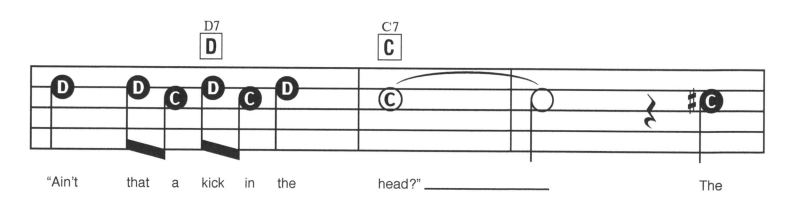

"Ain't that a kick in the head?" _____ The

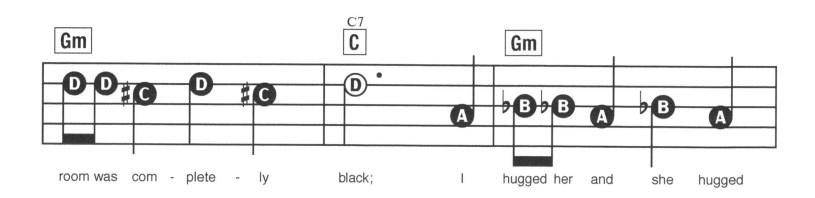

room was com-plete-ly black; I hugged her and she hugged

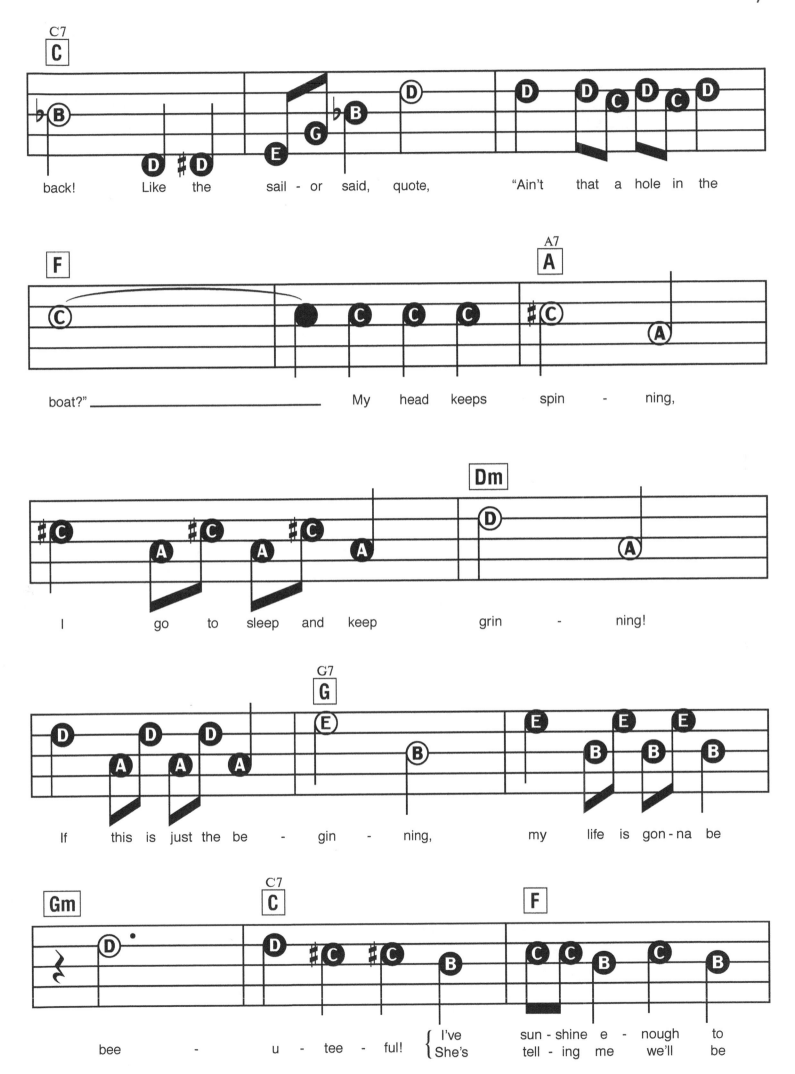

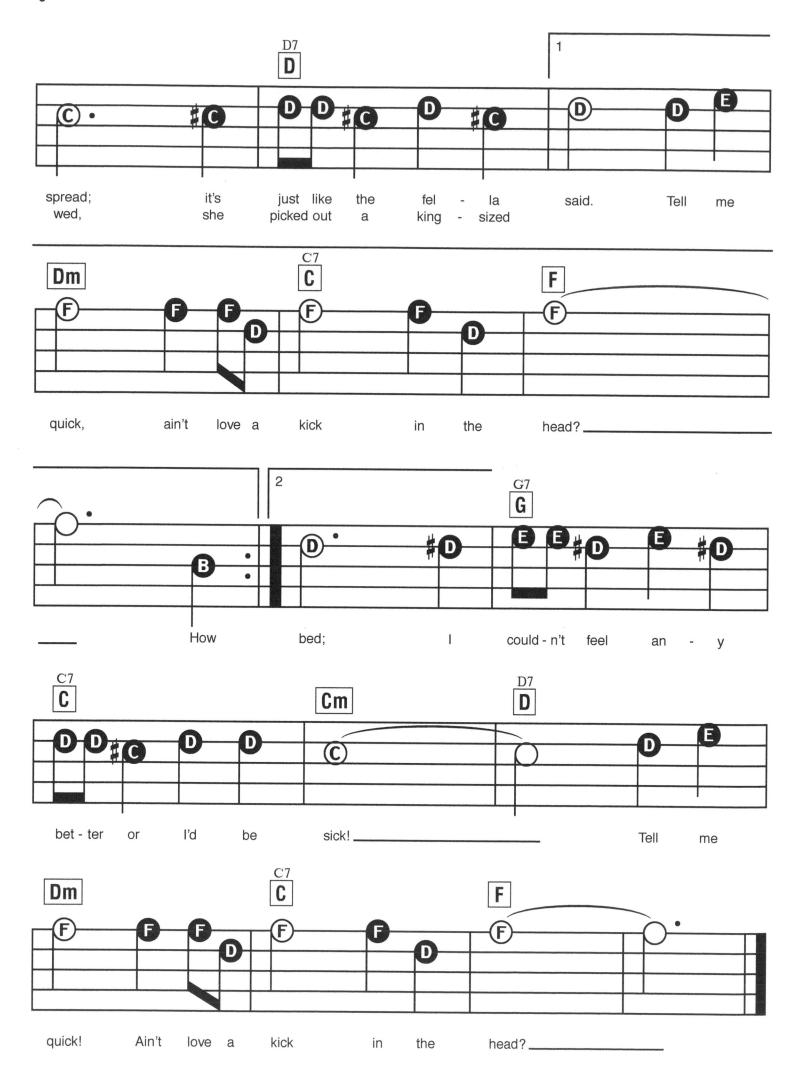

Too Close for Comfort
from the Musical MR. WONDERFUL

Registration 8
Rhythm: Swing

Words and Music by Jerry Bock,
Larry Holofcener and George Weiss

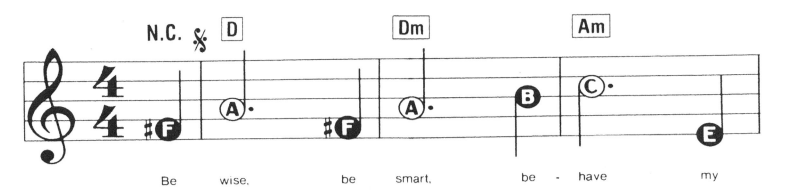

Be   wise,   be   smart,   be - have   my

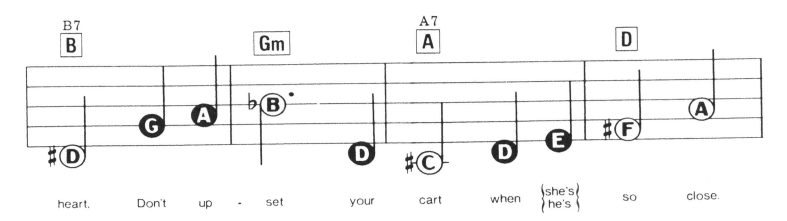

heart.   Don't   up - set   your   cart   when   {she's/he's}   so   close.

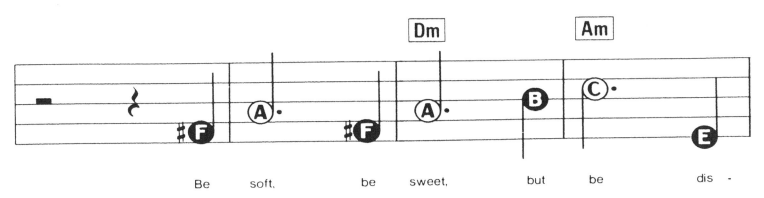

Be   soft,   be   sweet,   but   be   dis -

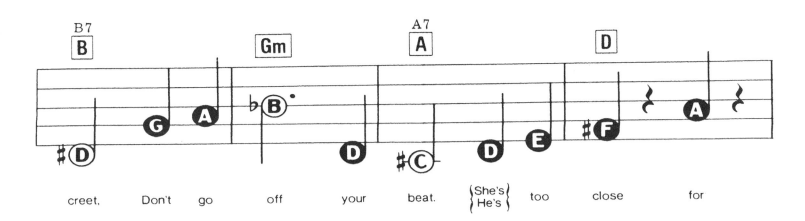

creet,   Don't   go   off   your   beat.   {She's/He's}   too   close   for

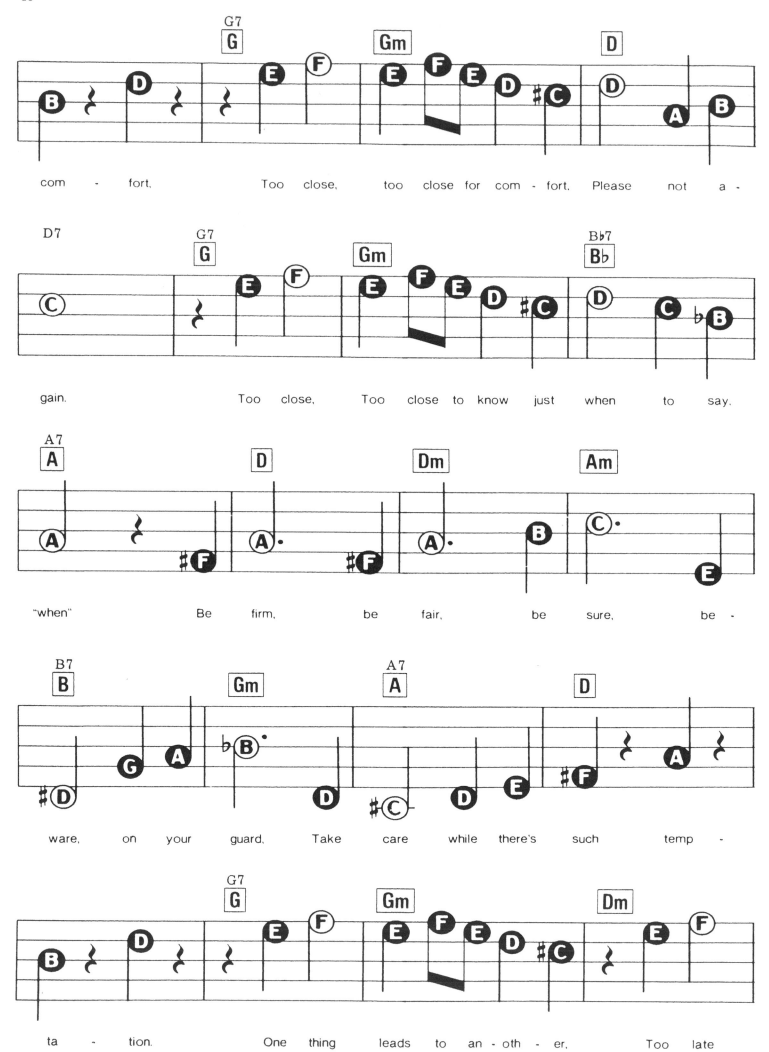

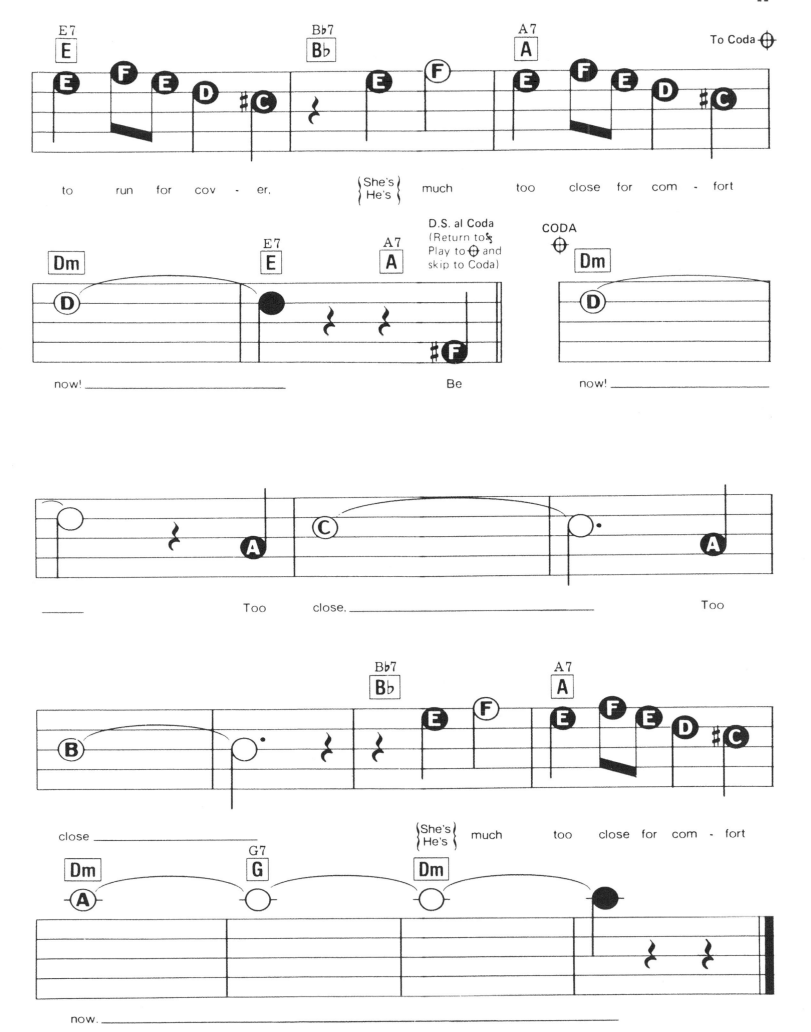

I've Got You Under My Skin

Registration 5
Rhythm: Ballad or Fox Trot

Words and Music by
Cole Porter

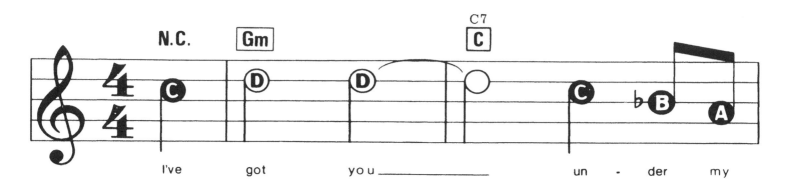

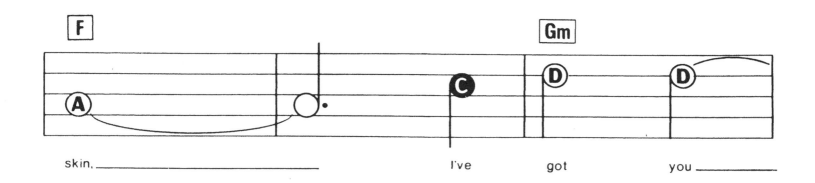

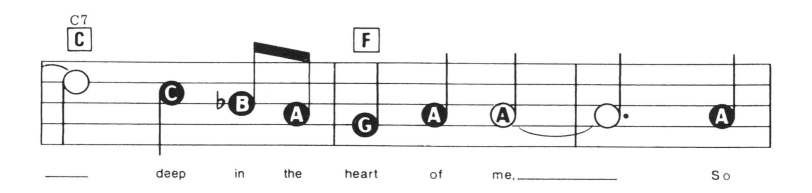

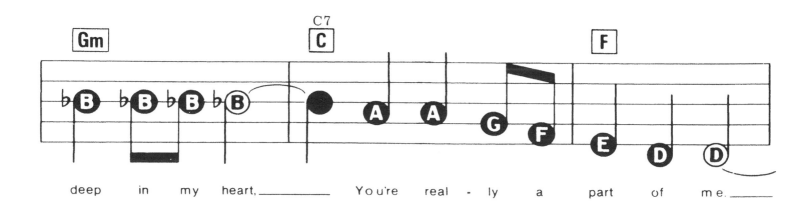

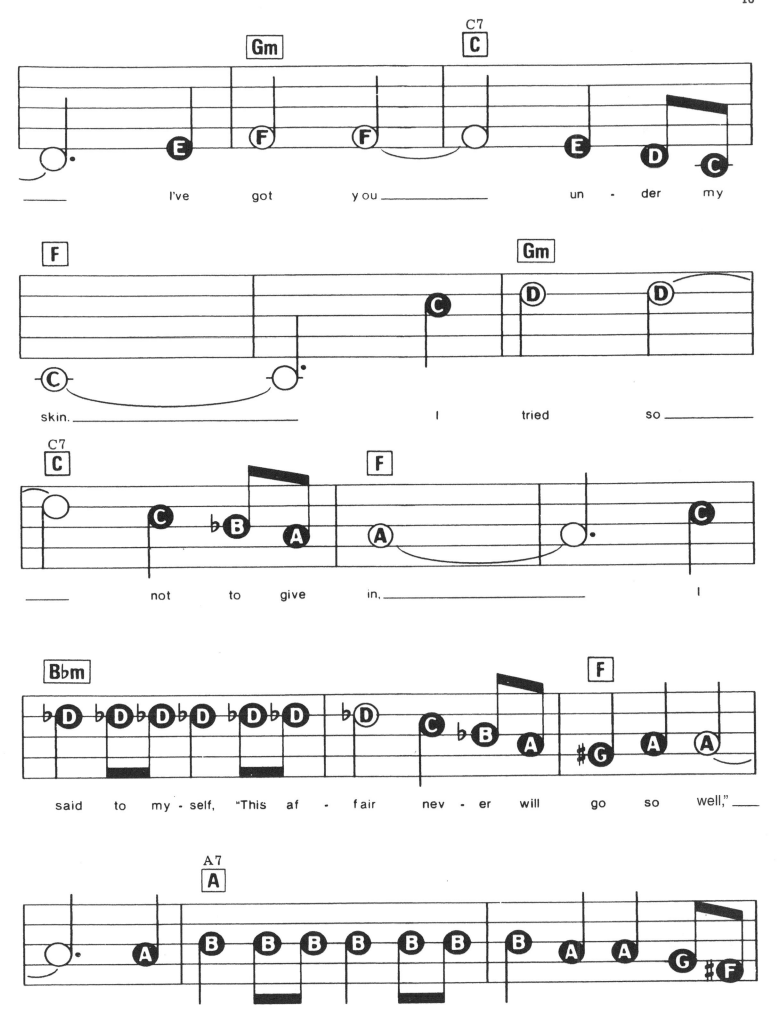

14

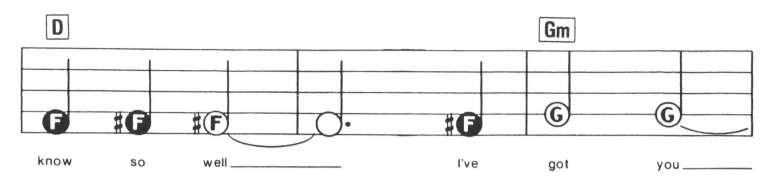

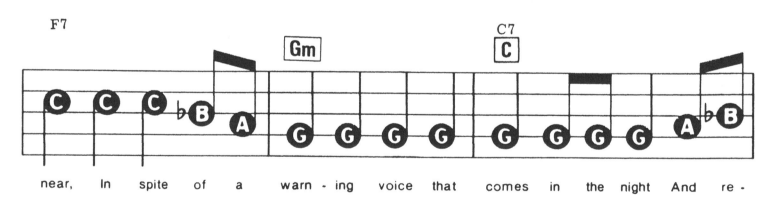

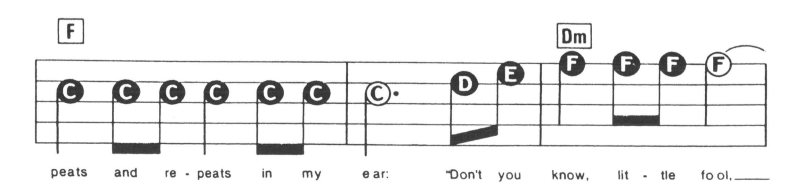

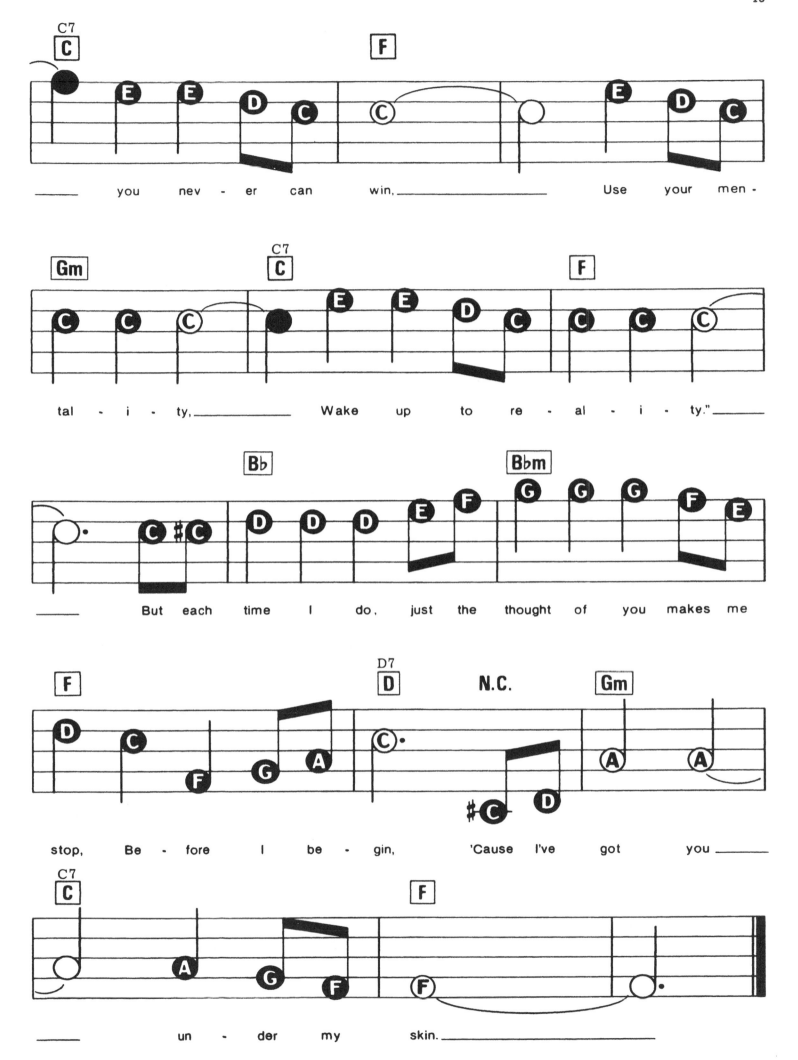

Who's Got the Action?

Registration 2
Rhythm: Swing or Fox Trot

Words and Music by George Duning
and Jack Brooks

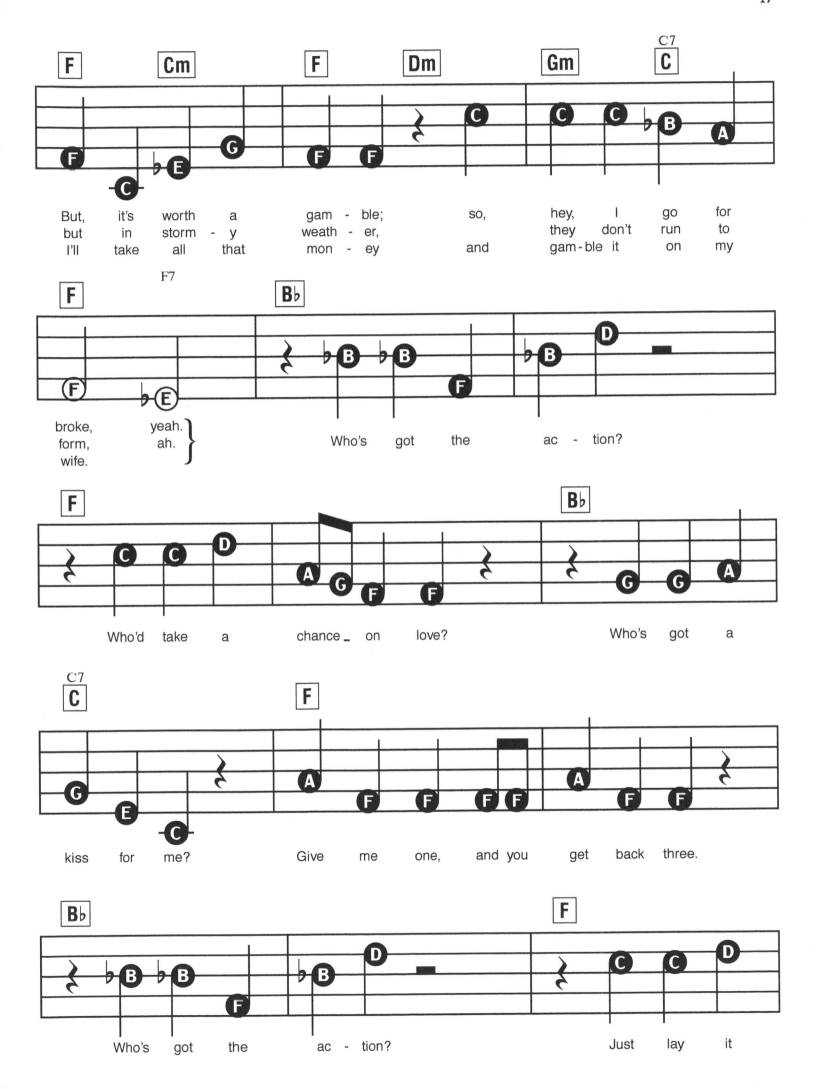

18

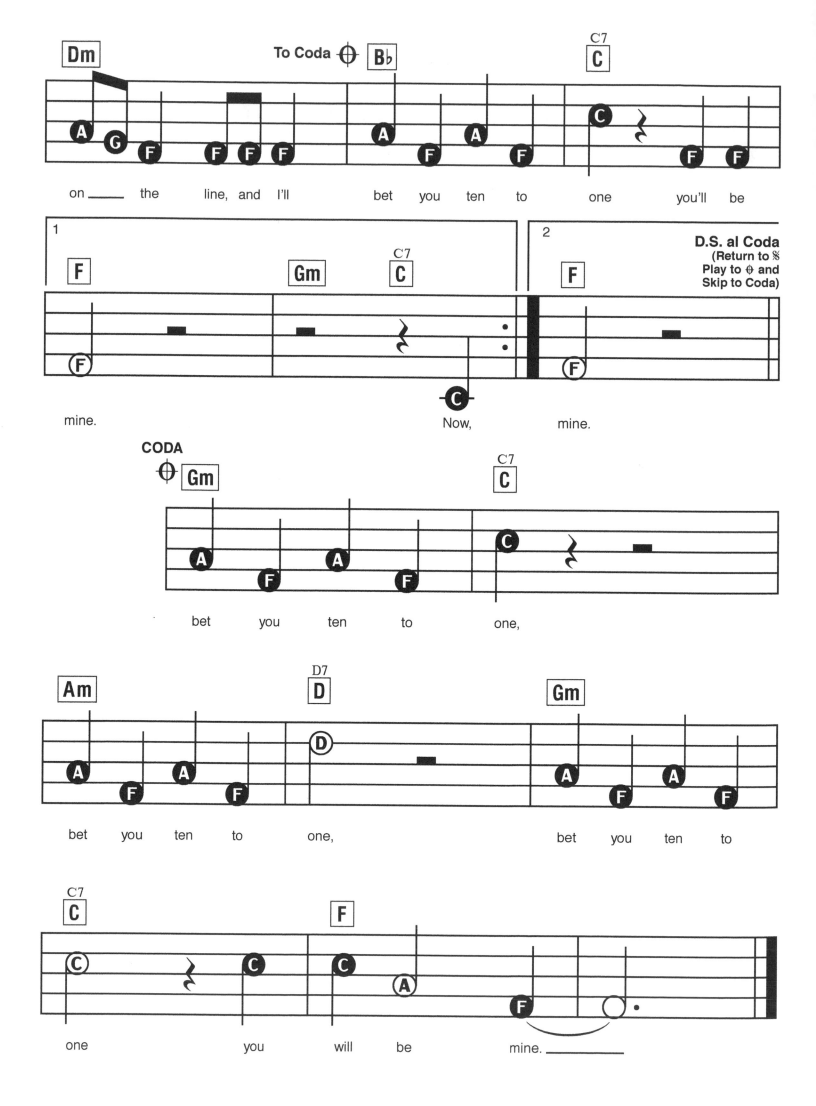

A Lot of Livin' To Do
from BYE BYE BIRDIE

Registration 2
Rhythm: Fox Trot or Swing

Lyric by Lee Adams
Music by Charles Strouse

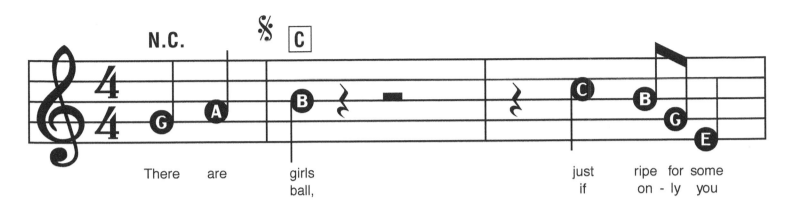

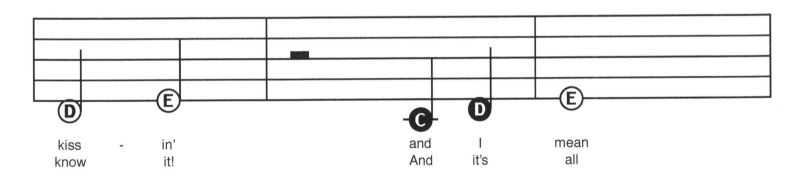

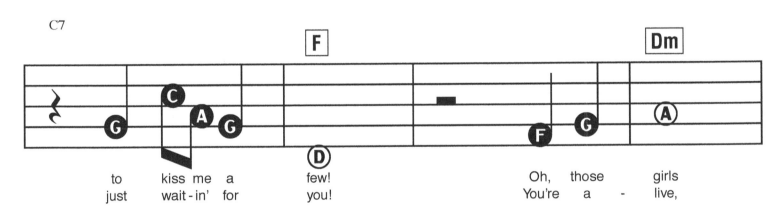

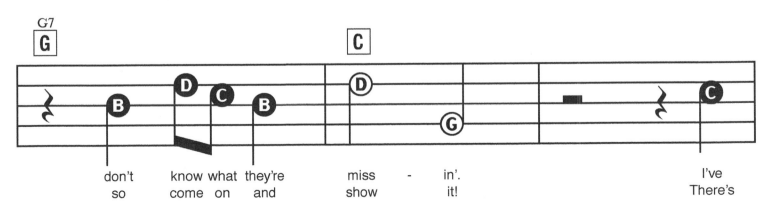

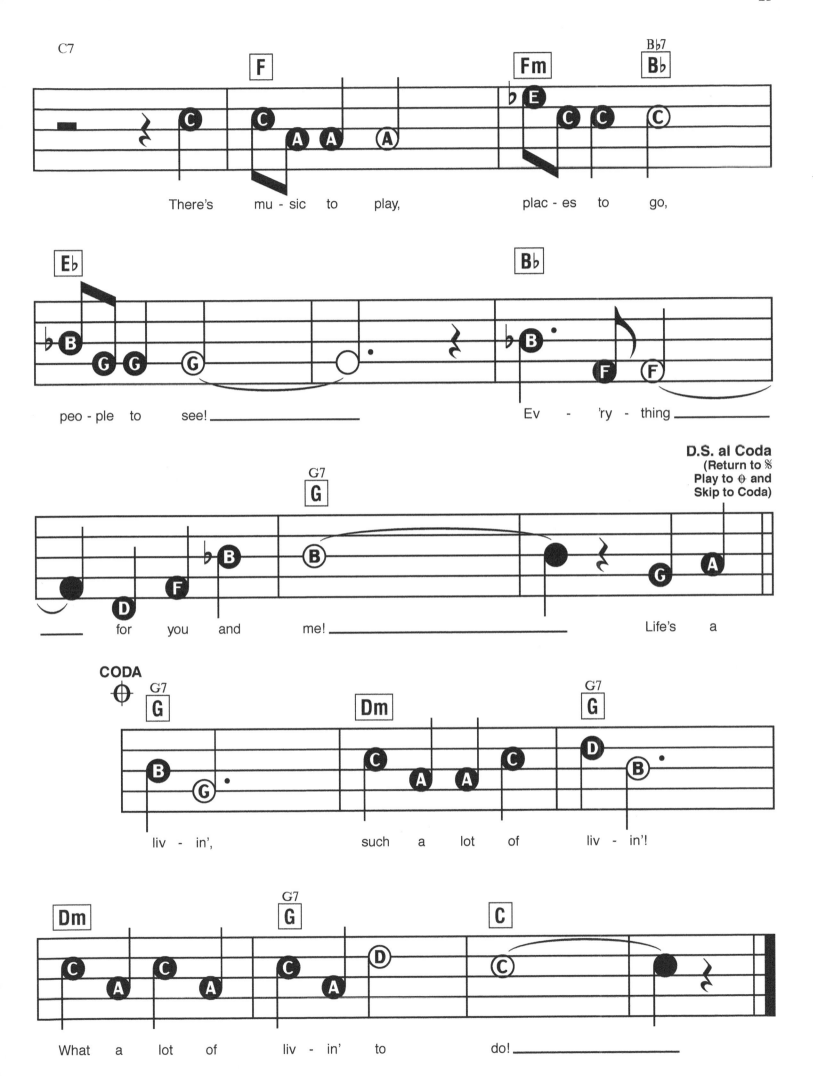

Ring-a-Ding Ding

Registration 3
Rhythm: Fox Trot or Swing

Words by Sammy Cahn
Music by James Van Heusen

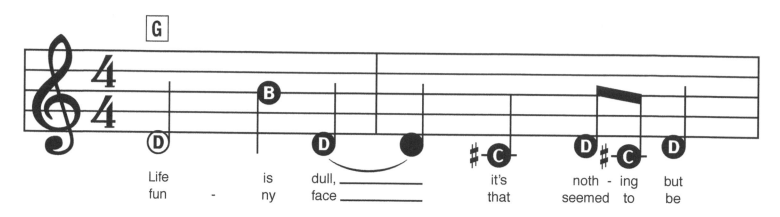

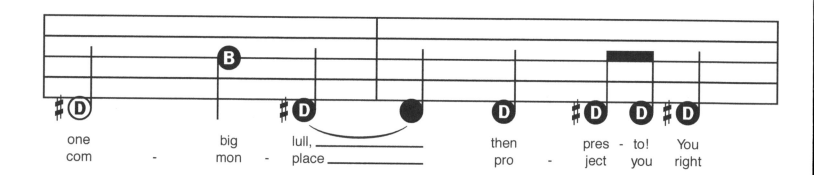

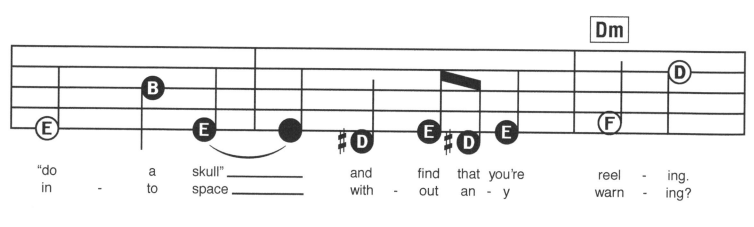

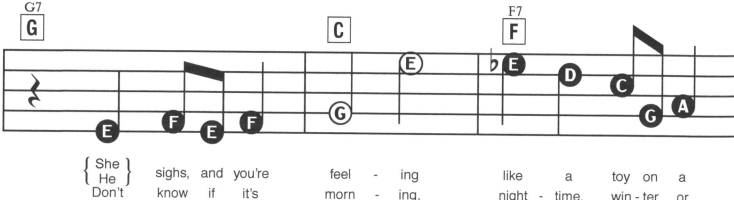

23

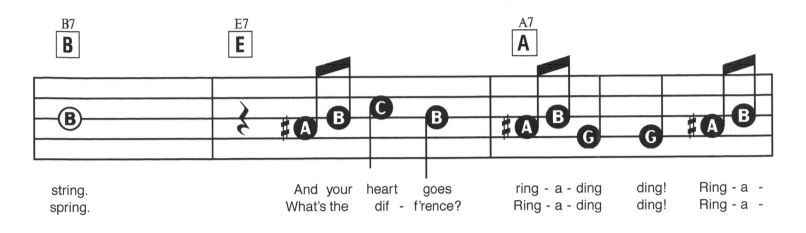

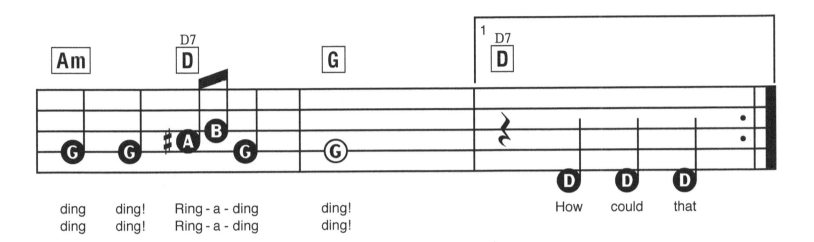

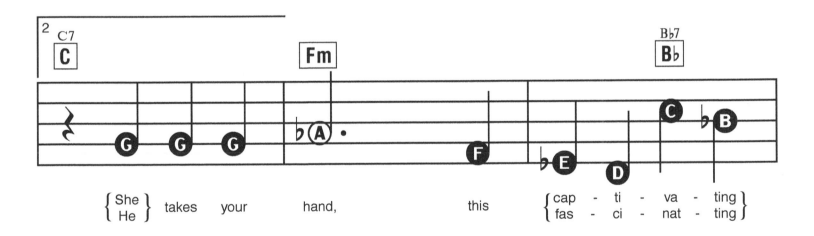

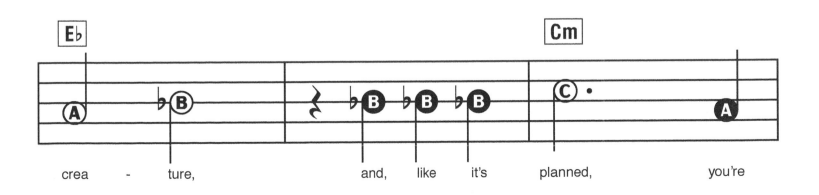

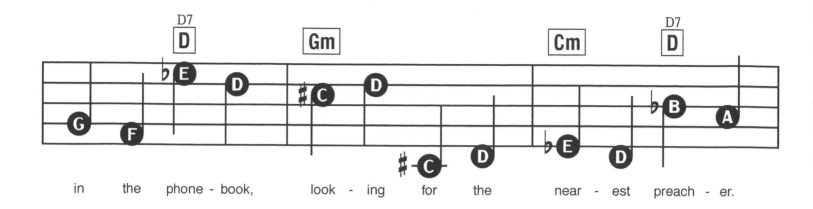

in the phone - book, look - ing for the near - est preach - er.

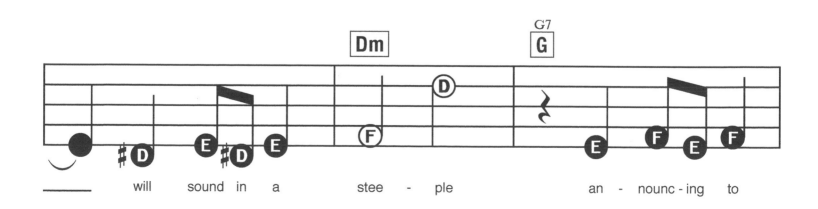

Life is swell, _____ you're off to that

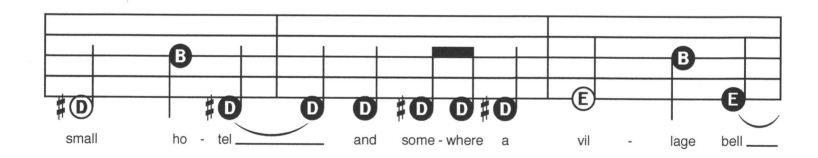

small ho - tel _____ and some - where a vil - lage bell _____

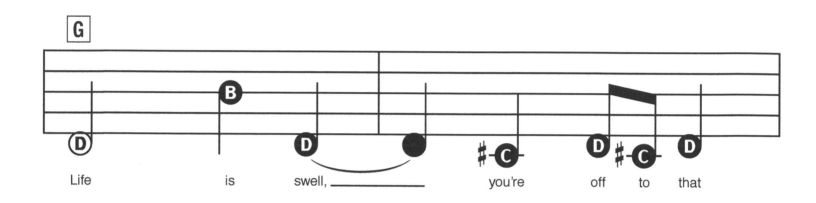

_____ will sound in a stee - ple an - nounc - ing to

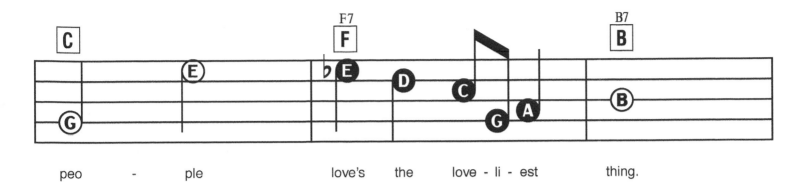

peo - ple love's the love - li - est thing.

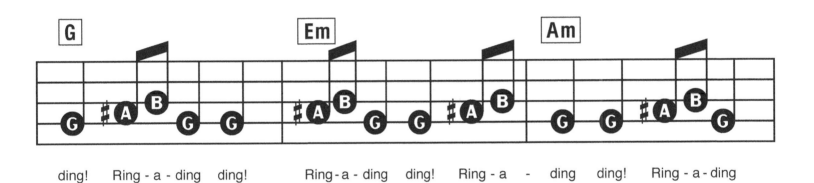

And the bell goes ring - a - ding ding! Ring - a - ding ding! Ring - a - ding

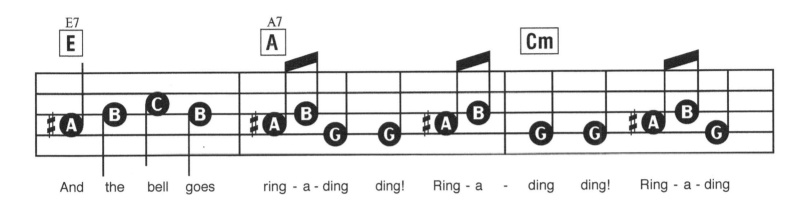

ding! Ring - a - ding ding! Ring - a - ding ding! Ring - a - ding ding! Ring - a - ding

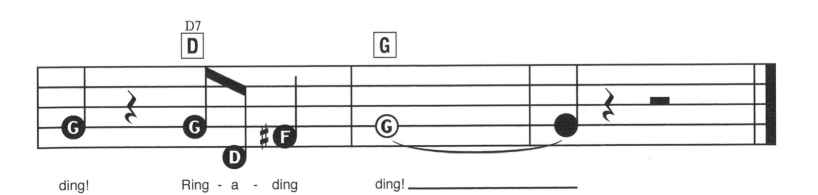

ding! Ring - a - ding ding! _____

EEE-O-Eleven

Registration 8
Rhythm: Swing or Fox Trot

Words by Sammy Cahn
Music by James Van Heusen

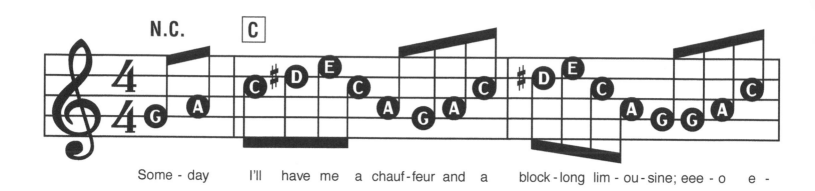

Some - day I'll have me a chauf-feur and a block-long lim-ou-sine; eee - o e -

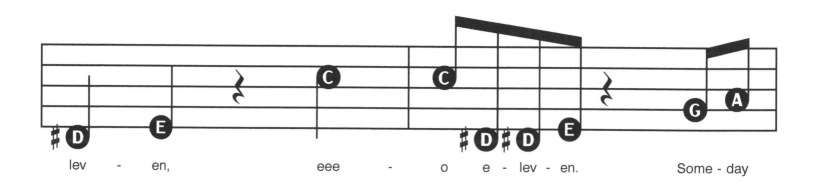

lev - en, eee - o e - lev - en. Some - day

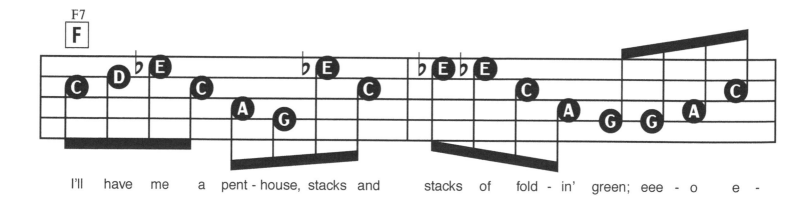

I'll have me a pent-house, stacks and stacks of fold-in' green; eee - o e -

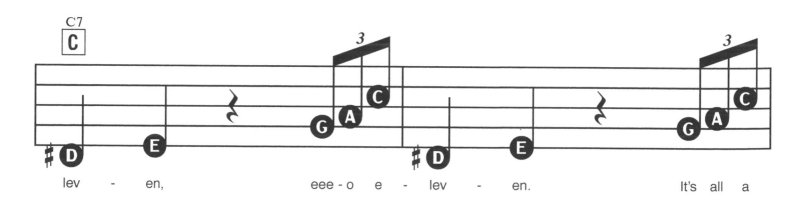

lev - en, eee-o e - lev - en. It's all a

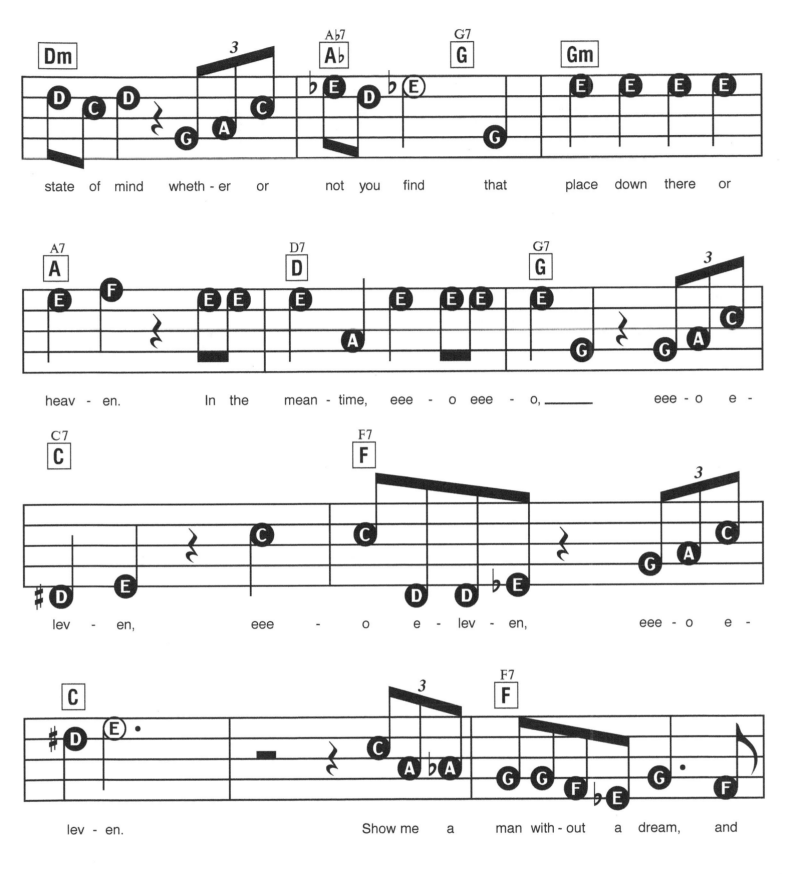

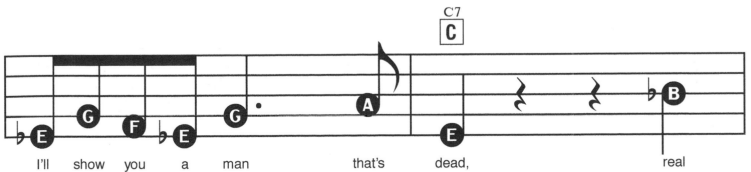

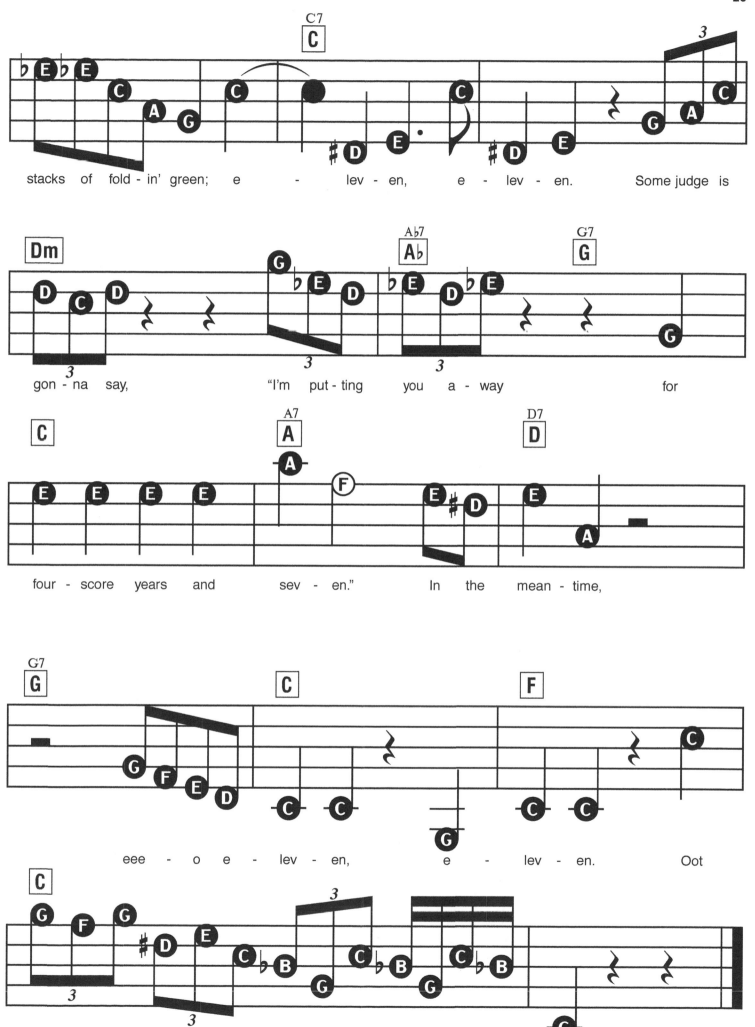

Luck Be a Lady
from GUYS AND DOLLS

Registration 4
Rhythm: Fox Trot or Swing

By Frank Loesser

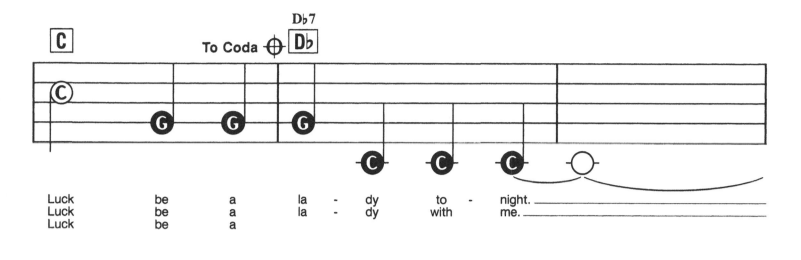

Luck be a la - dy to - night.
Luck be a a la - dy with me.
Luck be a

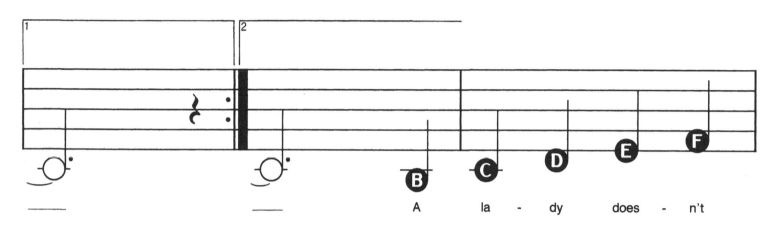

A la - dy does - n't

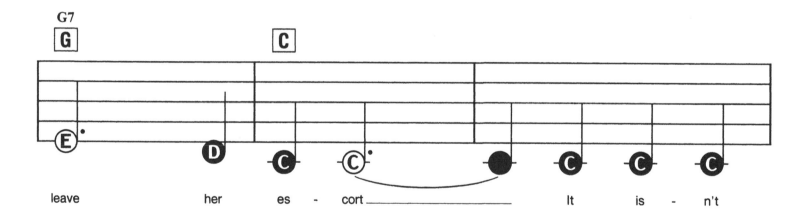

leave her es - cort It is - n't

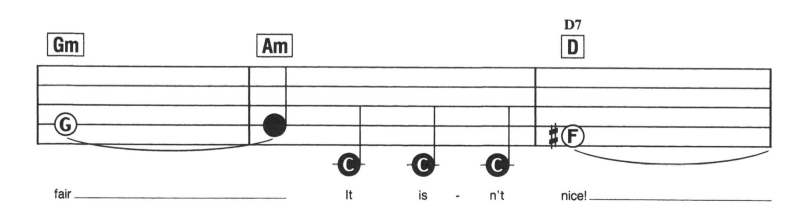

fair It is - n't nice!

32

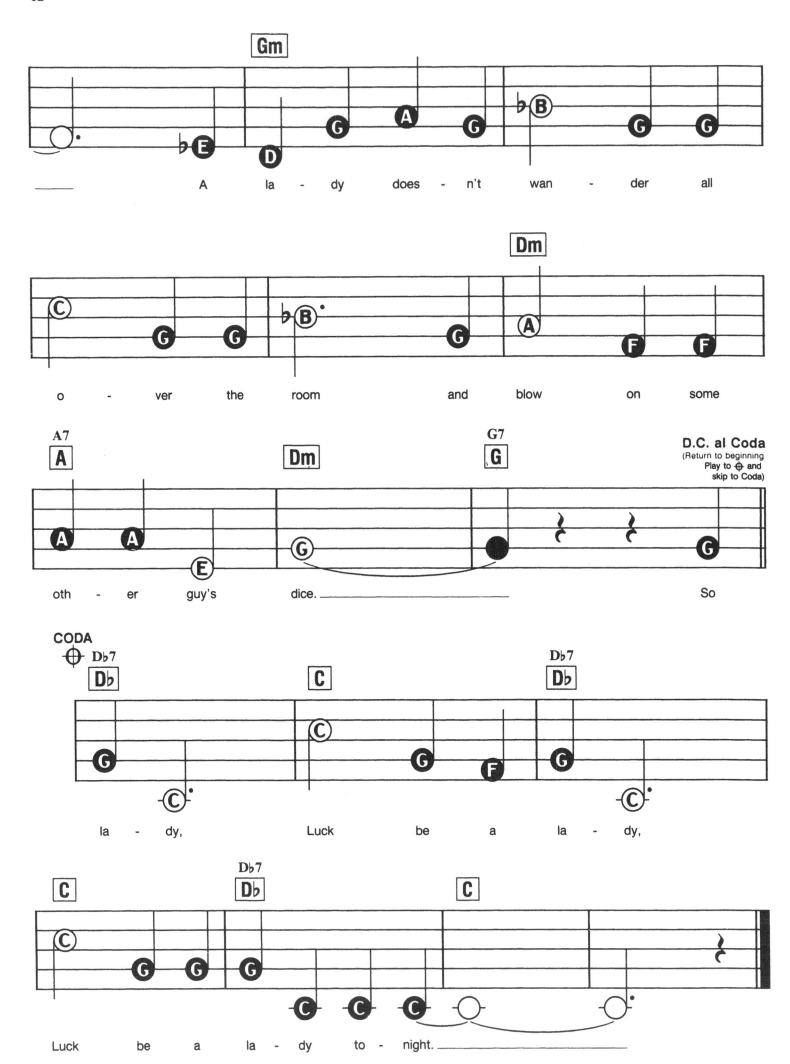

Volare
(Nel blu, dipinto di blu)

Registration 1
Rhythm: Swing

Music by Domenico Modugno
Original Italian Text by D. Modugno and F. Migliacci
English lyric by Mitchell Parish

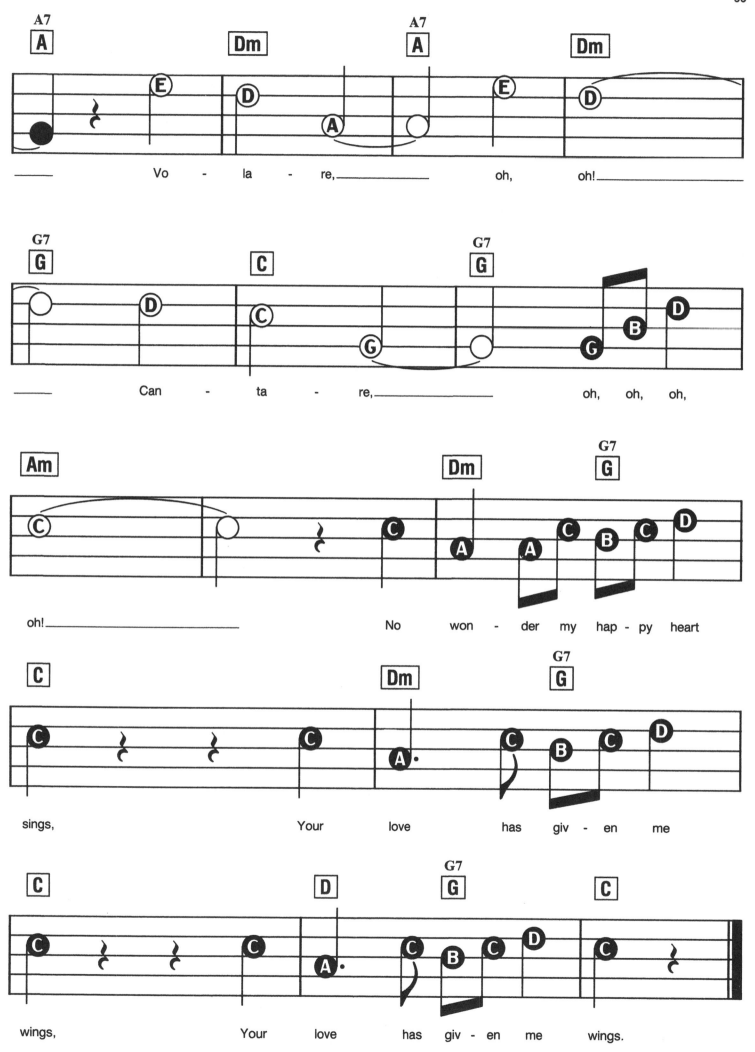

The Birth of the Blues
from GEORGE WHITE'S SCANDALS OF 1926

Registration 7
Rhythm: Fox Trot or Swing

Words by B.G. DeSylva and Lew Brown
Music by Ray Henderson

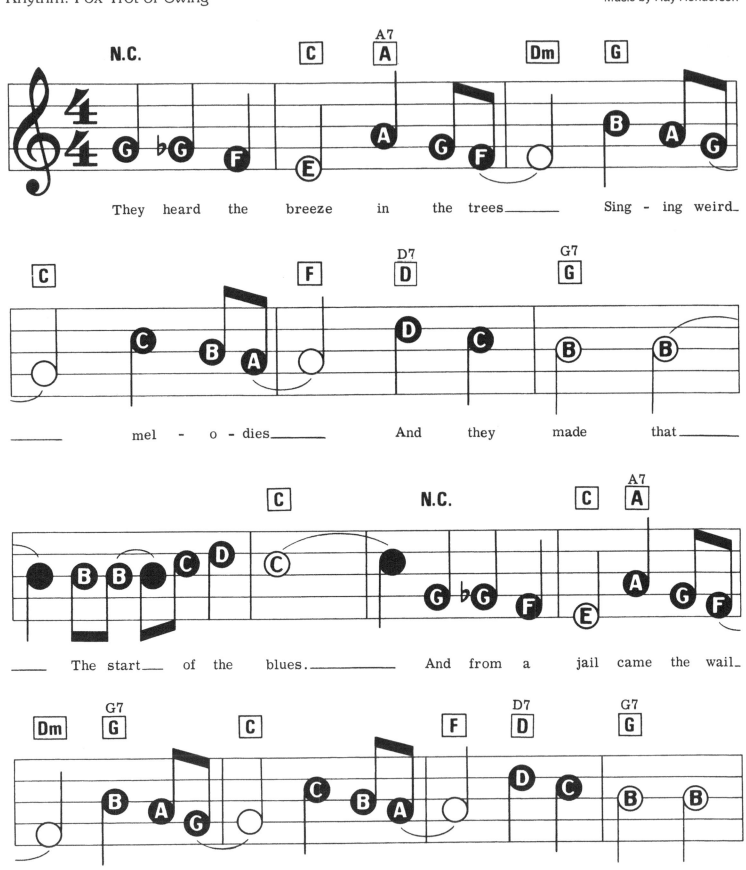

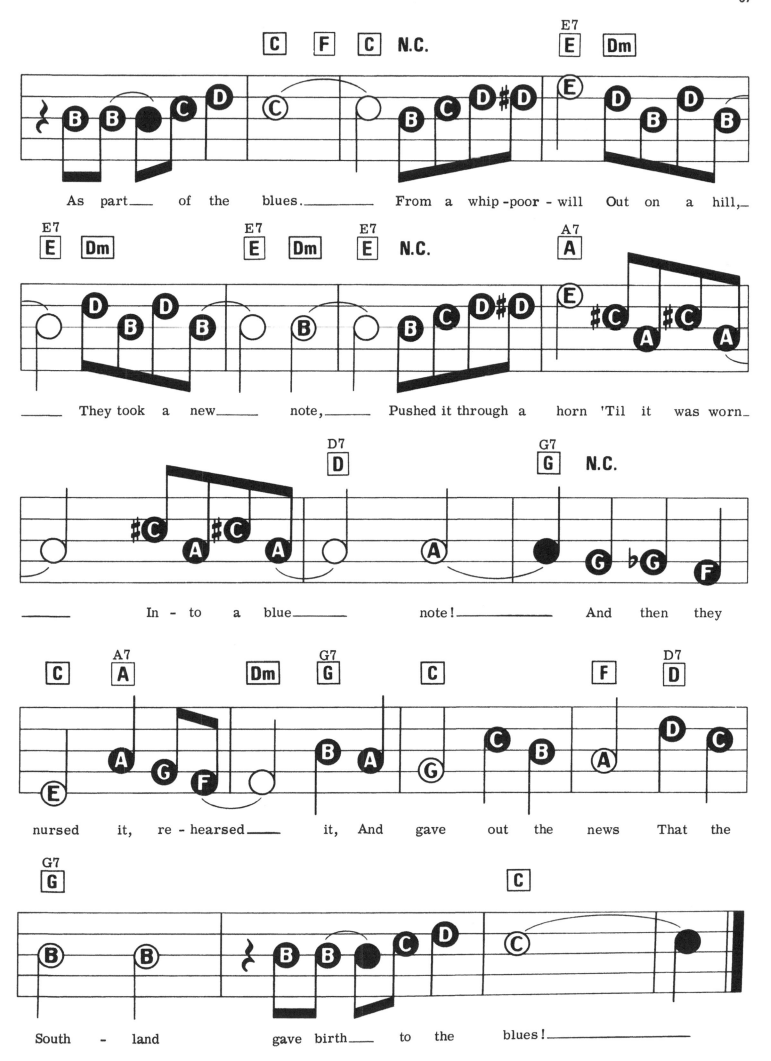

Witchcraft

Registration 9
Rhythm: Swing

Music by Cy Coleman
Lyrics by Carolyn Leigh

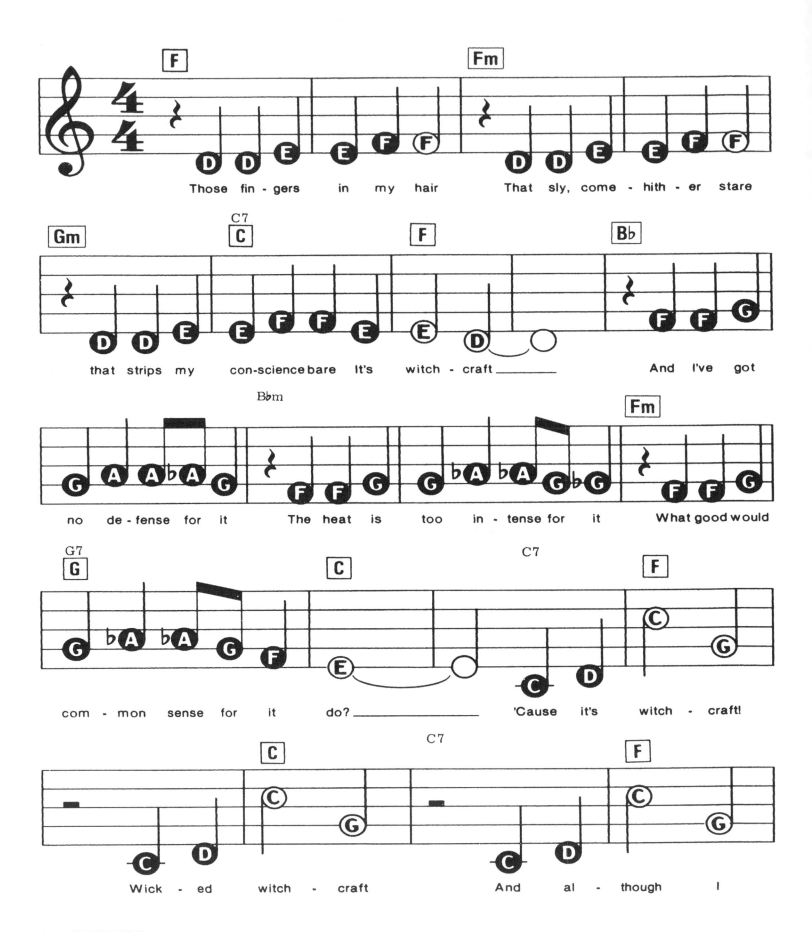

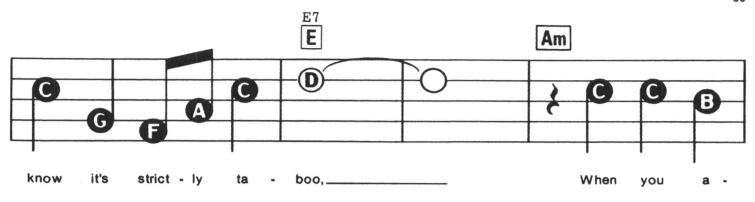

know it's strict - ly ta - boo,_____ When you a -

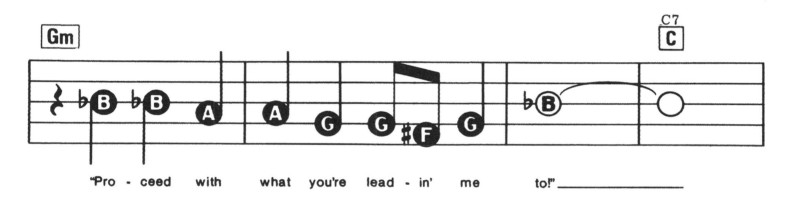

rouse the need in me, my heart says, "Yes, in - deed" in me,

"Pro - ceed with what you're lead - in' me to!"_____

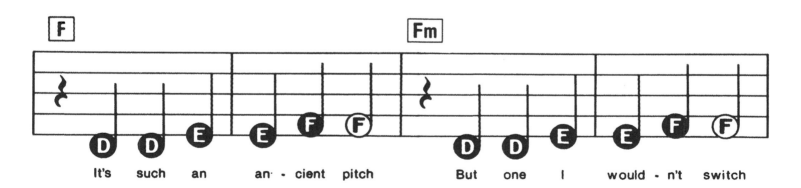

It's such an an - cient pitch But one I would - n't switch

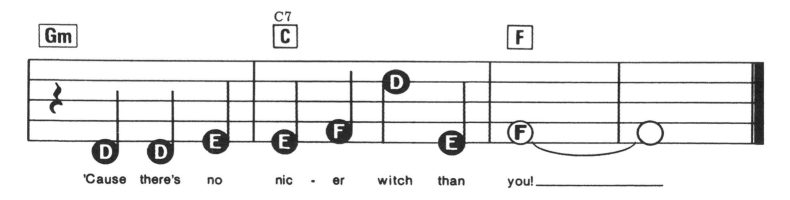

'Cause there's no nic - er witch than you!_____

You're Nobody
'til Somebody Loves You

Registration 2
Rhythm: Swing

Words and Music by Russ Morgan,
Larry Stock and James Cavanaugh

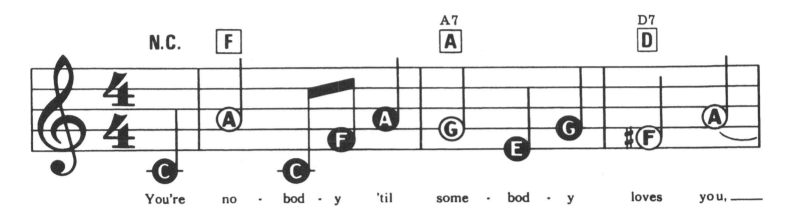

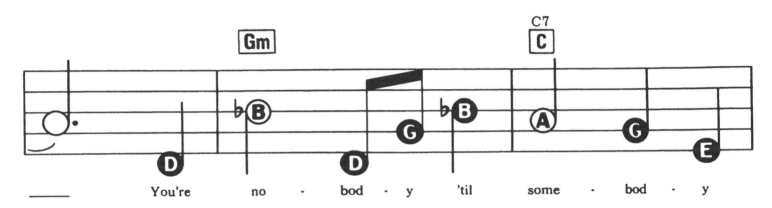

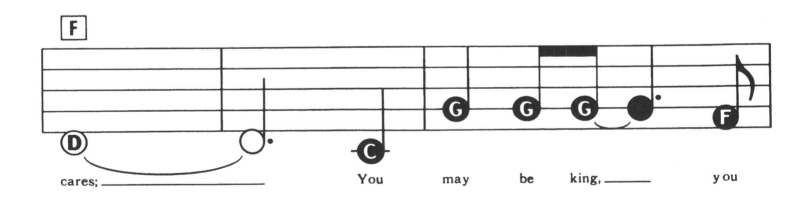

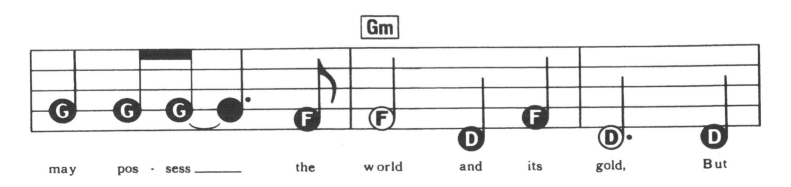

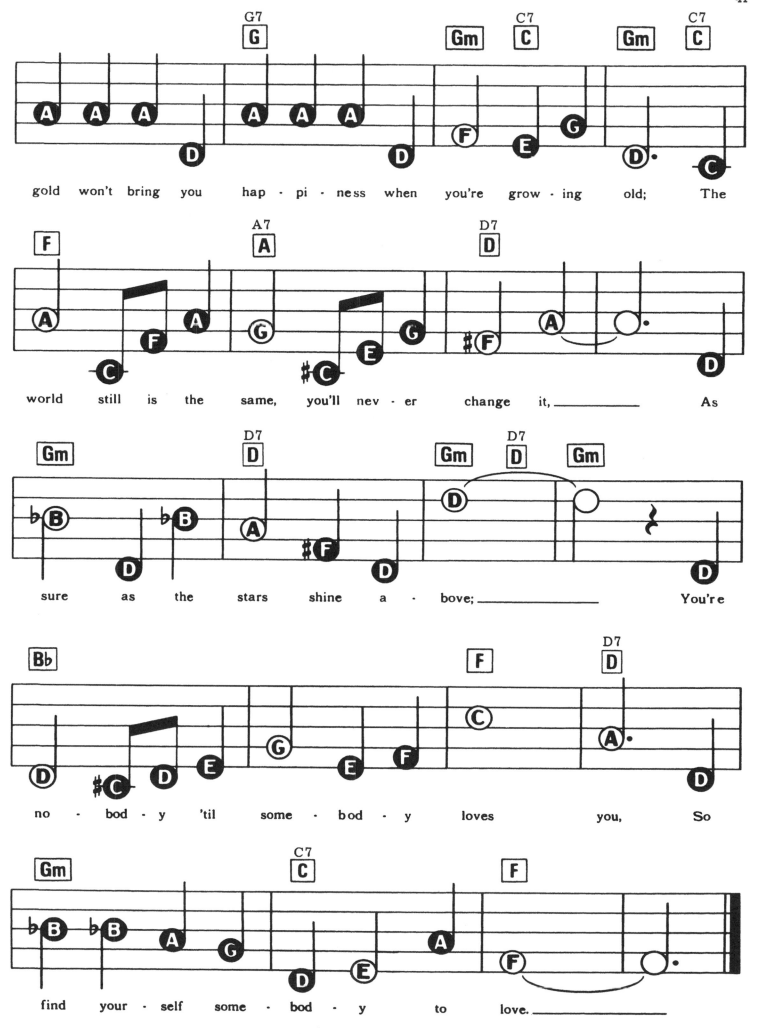

I Get a Kick Out of You
from ANYTHING GOES

Registration 4
Rhythm: Fox Trot or Swing

Words and Music by
Cole Porter

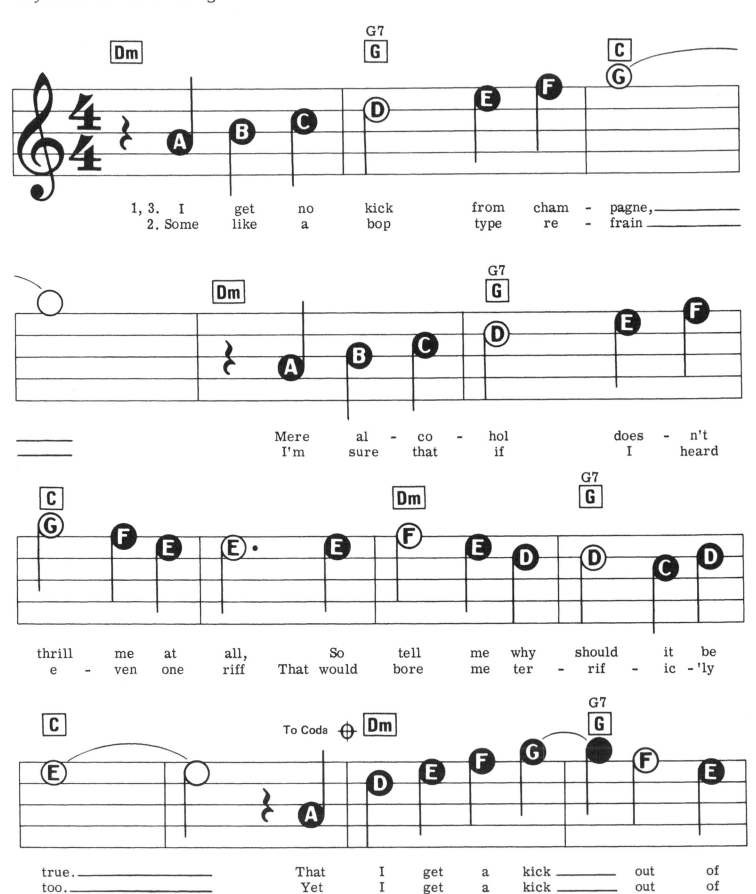

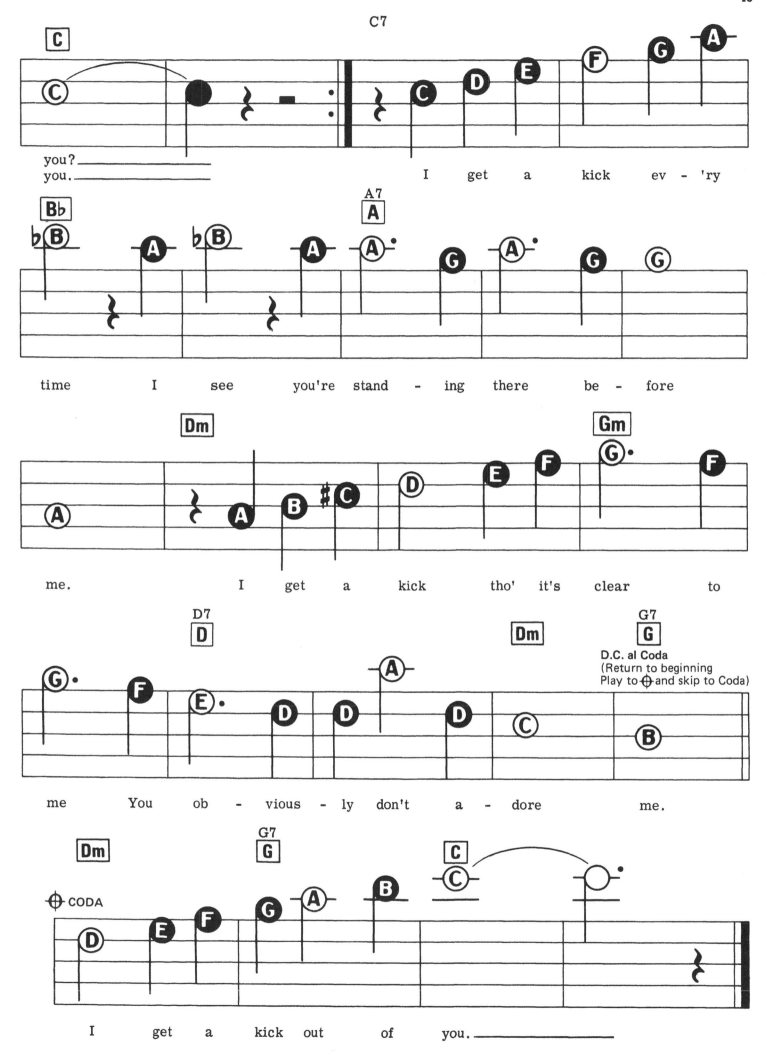

Sam's Song

Registration 8
Rhythm: Fox Trot or Swing

Words by Jack Elliott
Music by Lew Quadling

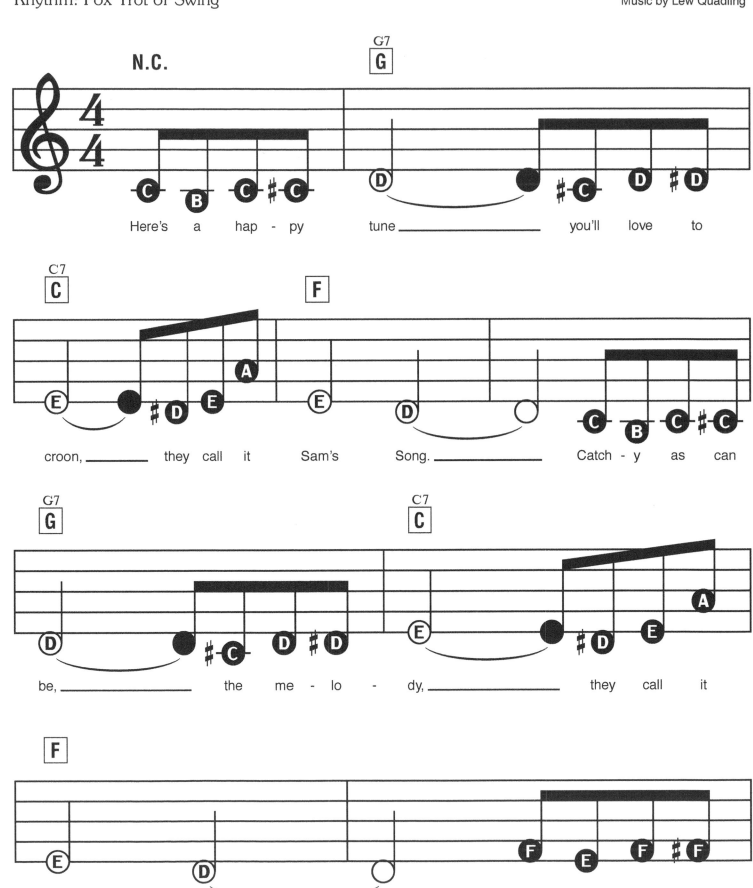

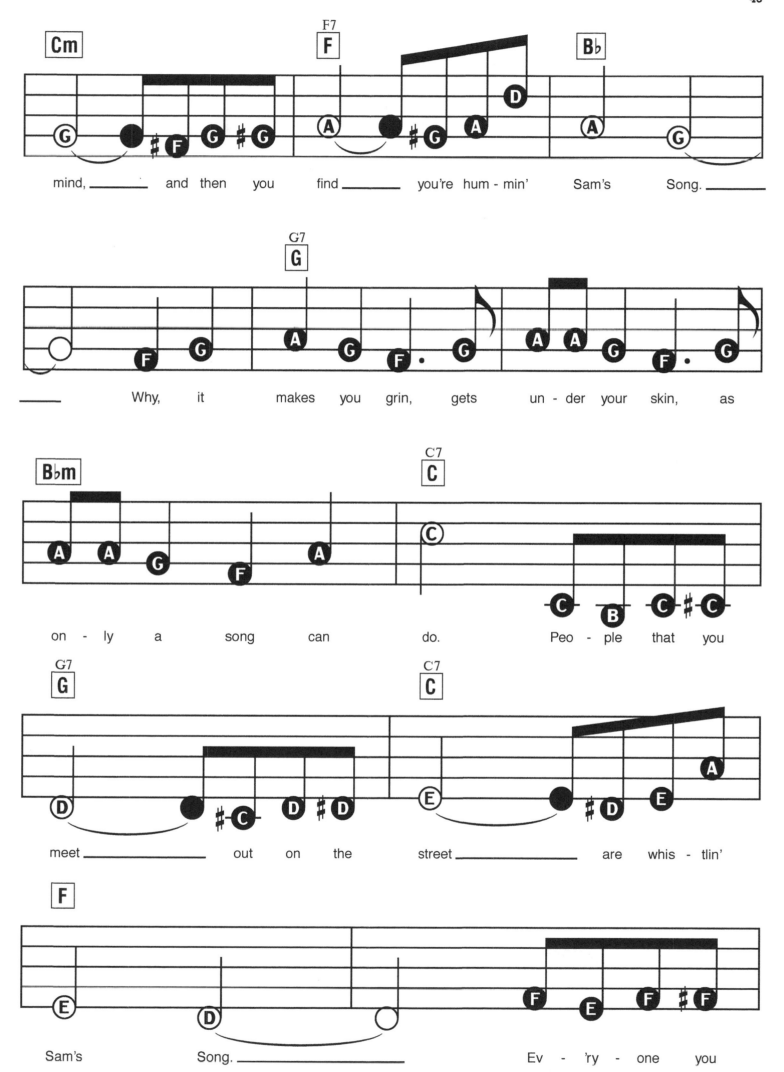

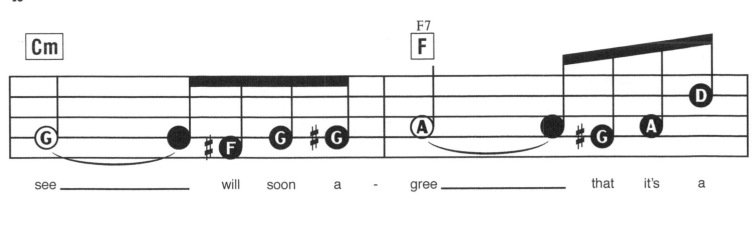

see _____ will soon a - gree _____ that it's a

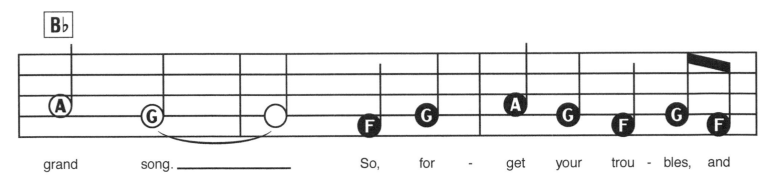

grand song. _____ So, for - get your trou - bles, and

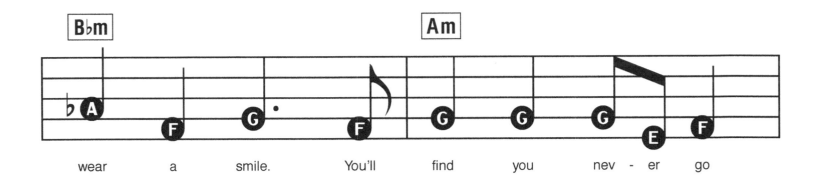

wear a smile. You'll find you nev - er go

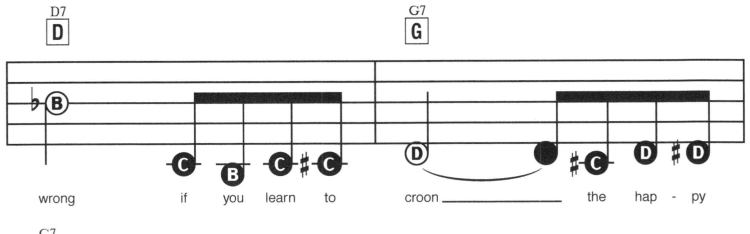

wrong if you learn to croon _____ the hap - py

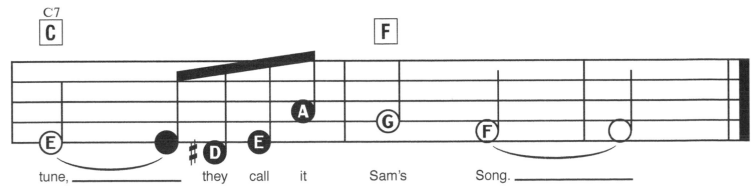

tune, _____ they call it Sam's Song. _____

I'm Gonna Live Till I Die

Registration 7
Rhythm: Swing

Words and Music by Al Hoffman,
Wlater Kent and Manny Kurtz

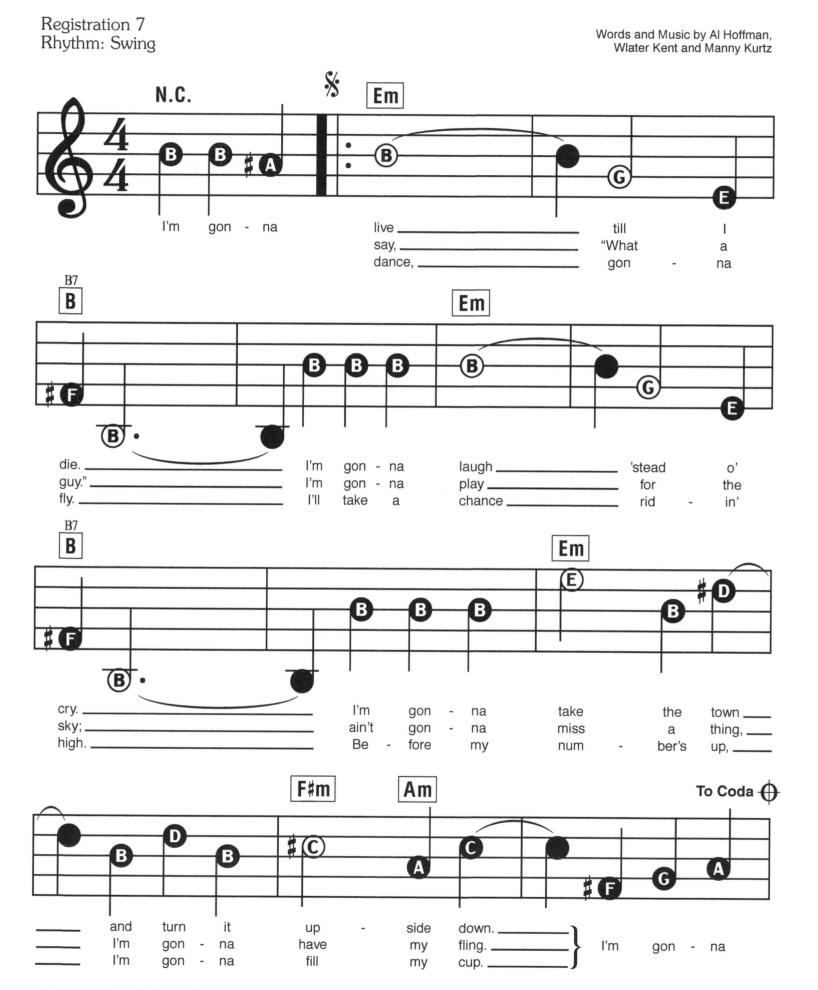

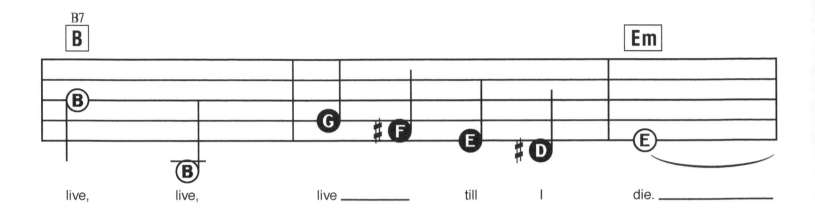

live, live, live _____ till I die. _____

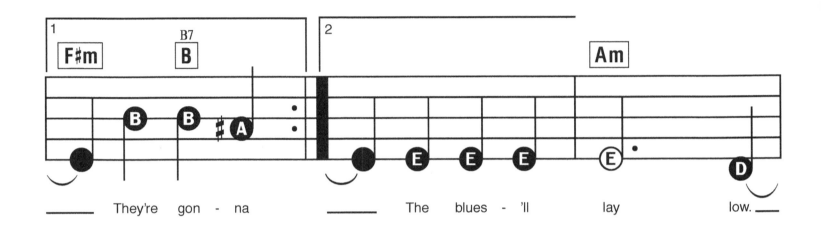

_____ They're gon - na _____ The blues - 'll lay low. __

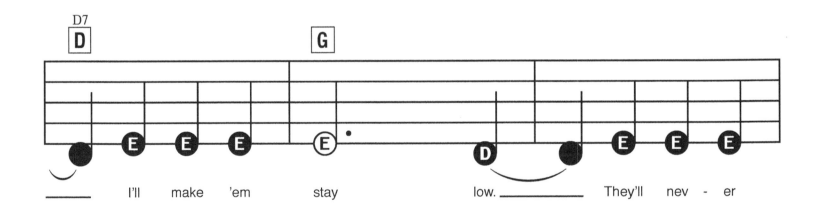

_____ I'll make 'em stay low. _____ They'll nev - er

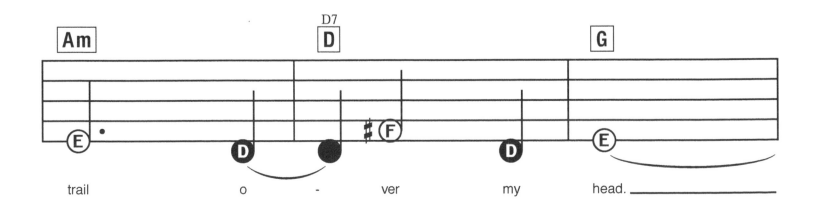

trail   o - ver my head. _____

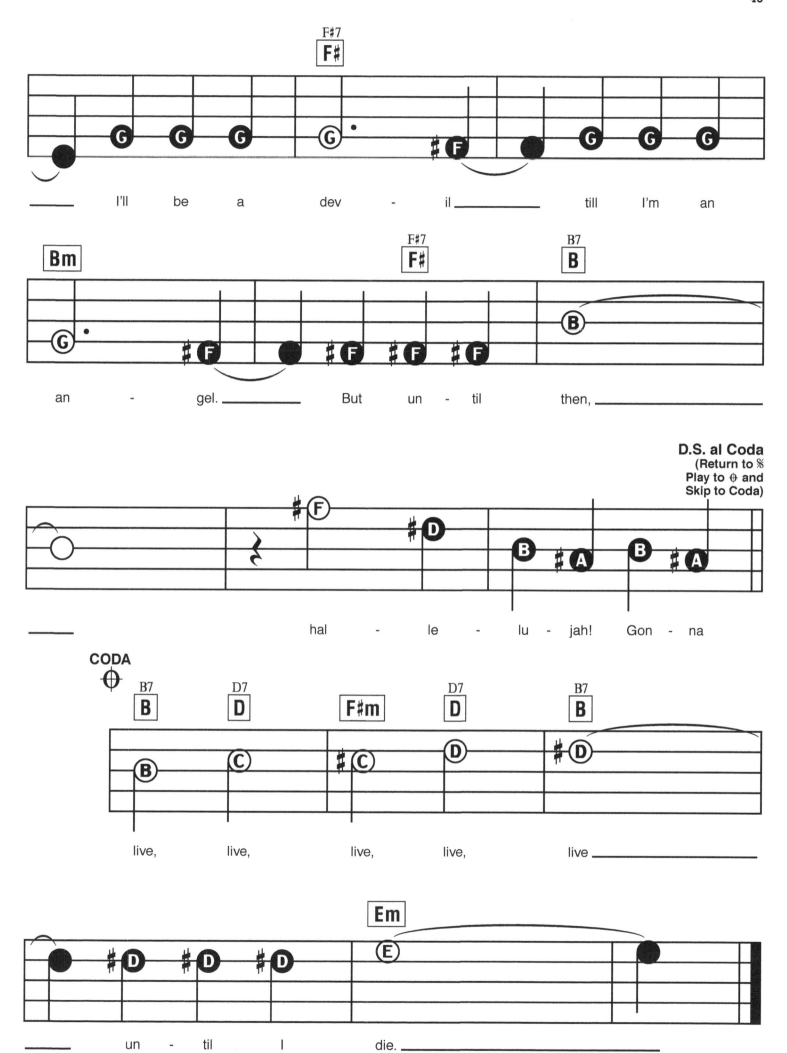

Me and My Shadow

Registration 1
Rhythm: Fox Trot

Words by Billy Rose
Music by Al Jolson and Dave Dreyer

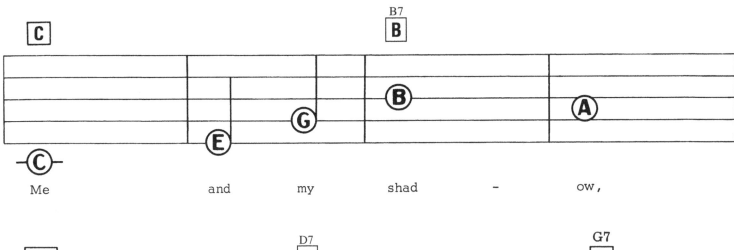

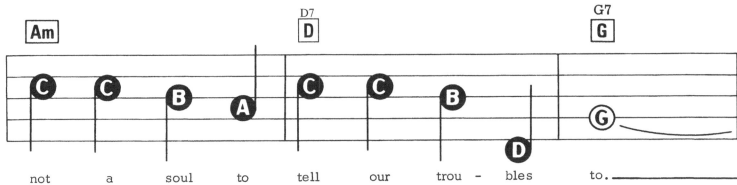

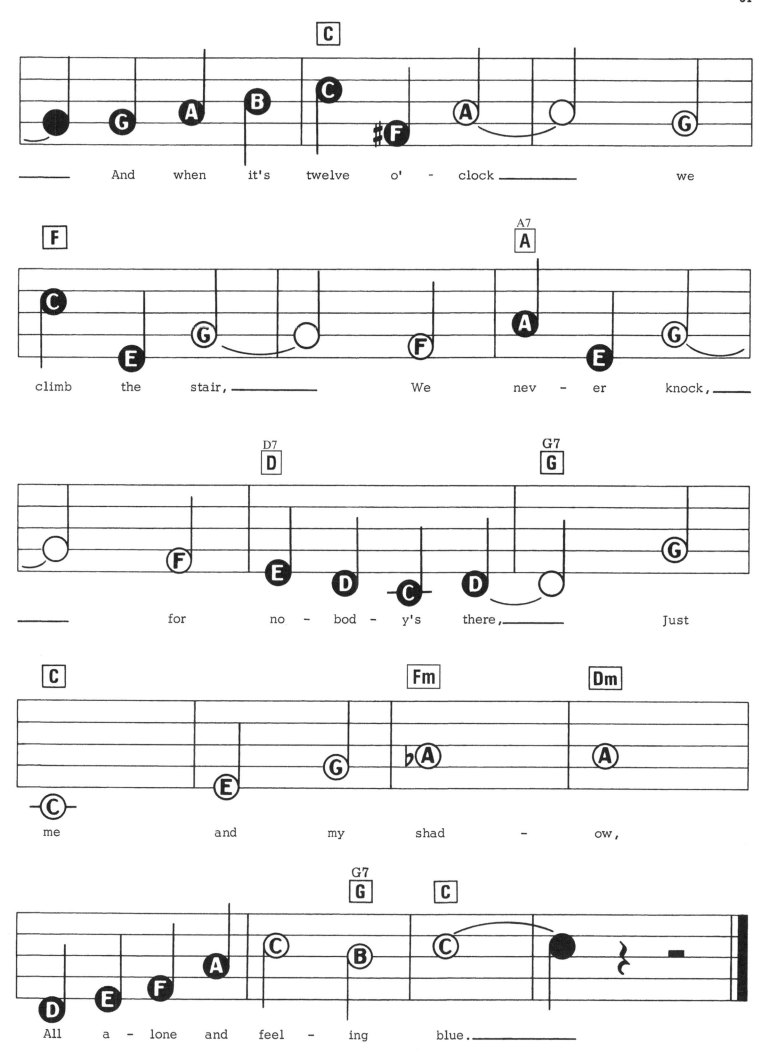

Everybody Loves Somebody

Registration 4
Rhythm: Swing or Shuffle

Words by Irving Taylor
Music by Ken Lane

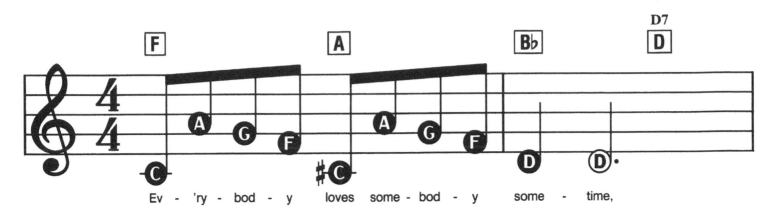

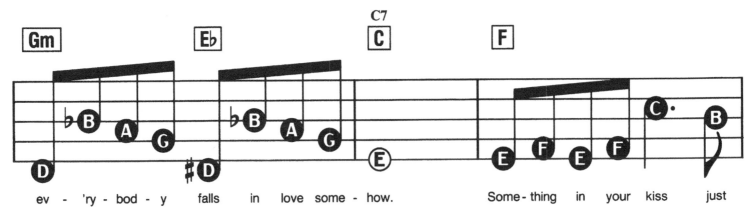

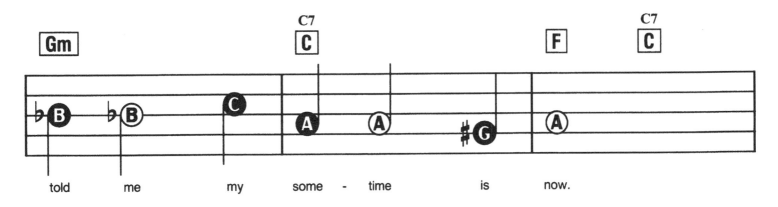

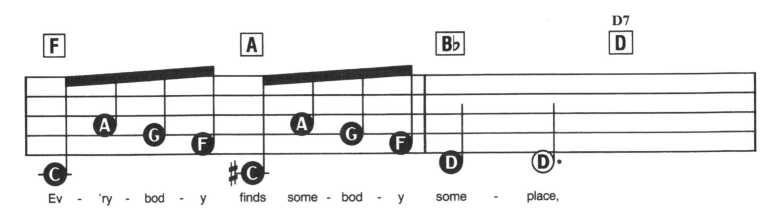

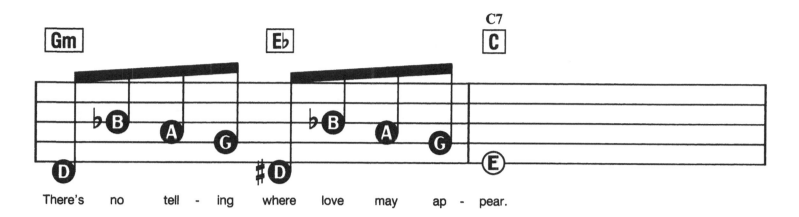

There's no tell - ing where love may ap - pear.

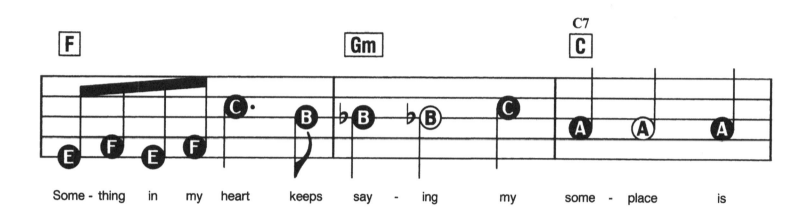

Some - thing in my heart keeps say - ing my some - place is

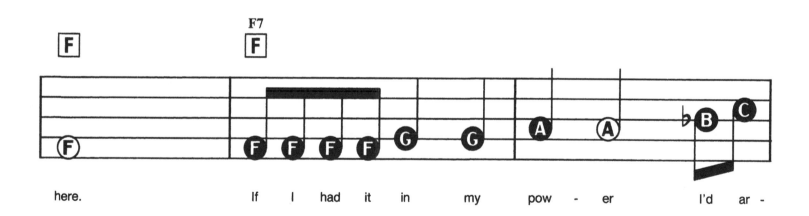

here. If I had it in my pow - er I'd ar -

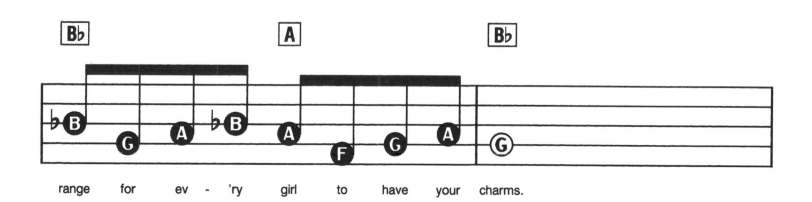

range for ev - 'ry girl to have your charms.

Registration Guide

• Match the Registration number on the song to the corresponding numbered category below. Select and activate an instrumental sound available on your instrument.

• Choose an automatic rhythm appropriate to the mood and style of the song. (Consult your Owner's Guide for proper operation of automatic rhythm features.)

• Adjust the tempo and volume controls to comfortable settings.

Registration

1	Mellow	Flutes, Clarinet, Oboe, Flugel Horn, Trombone, French Horn, Organ Flutes
2	Ensemble	Brass Section, Sax Section, Wind Ensemble, Full Organ, Theater Organ
3	Strings	Violin, Viola, Cello, Fiddle, String Ensemble, Pizzicato, Organ Strings
4	Guitars	Acoustic/Electric Guitars, Banjo, Mandolin, Dulcimer, Ukulele, Hawaiian Guitar
5	Mallets	Vibraphone, Marimba, Xylophone, Steel Drums, Bells, Celesta, Chimes
6	Liturgical	Pipe Organ, Hand Bells, Vocal Ensemble, Choir, Organ Flutes
7	Bright	Saxophones, Trumpet, Mute Trumpet, Synth Leads, Jazz/Gospel Organs
8	Piano	Piano, Electric Piano, Honky Tonk Piano, Harpsichord, Clavi
9	Novelty	Melodic Percussion, Wah Trumpet, Synth, Whistle, Kazoo, Perc. Organ
10	Bellows	Accordion, French Accordion, Mussette, Harmonica, Pump Organ, Bagpipes